The Japanese Association for South Asian Studies
Established in 1988

- **Office Bearers as of 1 November 2006**

  President
  Hiroshi Ishii, Professor Emeritus, Tokyo University of Foreign Studies

  General Secretary
  Shingo Einoo, University of Tokyo

  Members of the Board of Executive Directors
  Norio Kondo, Institute of Developing Economies
  Yoshifumi Mizuno, Tokyo University of Foreign Studies
  Tsukasa Mizushima, University of Tokyo
  Fumiko Oshikawa, Kyoto University
  Masahiro Shimoda, University of Tokyo
  Akio Tanabe, Kyoto University
  Shinkichi Taniguchi, Hitotsubashi University
  Kohei Wakimura, Osaka City University

- **Head Office** (until September 2008)
  c/o Institute of Oriental Culture, University of Tokyo
  7-3-1 Hongo, Bunkyo-ku, Tokyo, 113-0033, Japan
  Fax. +81-3-5841-5898
  Email. jasas@ioc.u-tokyo.ac.jp
  http://wwwsoc.nii.ac.jp/jasas/index-e.html

- **Publications in English**
  1 *JJASAS (Journal of the Japanese Association for South Asian Studies)*, (annual publication in Japanese and English, the current issue: No. 18)
  2 Japanese Studies on South Asia Series
    No. 1 H. Kotani ed., *Caste System, Untouchability and the Depressed,* Manohar, New Delhi, 1997.
    No. 2 N. Karashima ed., *Kingship in Indian History*, Manohar, New Delhi, 1999.
    No. 3 S. Maeda ed., *The Way to Liberation*, Manohar, New Delhi, 2000.
    No. 4 S. Einoo and J. Takashima eds., *From Material to Deity*, Manohar, New Delhi, 2005.
    No. 5 H. Okahashi ed., *Emerging New Industrial Spaces and Regional Developments in India*, Manohar, New Delhi, 2008.

Japanese Studies on South Asia No. 5

EMERGING NEW INDUSTRIAL SPACES AND REGIONAL DEVELOPMENTS IN INDIA

Edited by

HIDENORI OKAHASHI

MANOHAR
2008

Tables

Acknowledgements

In 1989, I visited a village in the Vindhya Range in central India for work on a drought-prone area research project represented by Kenzo Fujiwara of Hiroshima University. On the way from Indore to the research site, we came upon a massive industrial estate in the wide open plateau country. It was the Pithampur Industrial Growth Centre. There, a new industrial agglomeration was beginning to take form, and with the aim of becoming India's Detroit, automotive related corporations such as small truck manufacturer (then known as) Eicher Mitsubishi and motorcycle manufacturer (then known as) Kinetic Honda were starting operations in plants that had just been constructed. It was this chance meeting that later would jump-start the development and fruition of a project to research the new development of industrialisation in India after economic liberalisation. In the three years between 1996 and 1998, I was fortunate to receive research grants from Japan's Ministry of Education, Culture, Sports, Science and Technology, allowing me to revisit Pithampur Industrial Growth Centre and conduct extensive field studies on a large number of staff and assistants. Also, I was able to carry out similar studies in NOIDA, a suburb of Delhi. This book is the result of geographic research on two large-scale industrial estates in north India which was made possible through these developments.

The late Professor Jiro Yonekura was the founder of Hiroshima University's regional geographic research on India. As a result of his tireless efforts, the first research project, 'Recent Changes in Settlements in India', was completed in 1967. Since then, geographic research on India through fieldwork has been continued by leaders such as Professors Hiroshi Ishida, Kenzo Fujiwara and Makoto Murakami, with nearly 40 years of research history between them. Research on India has been done in six project phases totalling a respectable sixteen times. During this period, the Indian government always supported our research and accommodated us with research visas. Also, we were greatly assisted by our joint researchers in India who devoted themselves to performing

Acknowledgements

CHAPTER 1

Introduction

HIDENORI OKAHASHI

OBJECTIVE

The objective of this book is to take a comprehensive look at regional development and regional change in India since economic liberalisation, with a focus on spaces where industrialisation is occurring: industrial estates. We focus on industrial estates not simply because we are interested in the advance of industrialisation, but because the formation of new industrial agglomerations, growth of suburban spaces, and re-development of neighbouring areas are intimately related to the growth of metropolitan areas and the transformation of a region. Industrial estates are in fact viewed as key to regarding change in India brought on by globalisation.

India's economy has been undergoing gradual liberalisation since the 1980s, but with a 'new economic policy' in 1991 that raised India's economy to the next level of openness to the world market, direct investment from overseas would immerse the Indian economy deep into globalisation. Naturally, the rate of industrialisation increased, and India entered into a new age of industrialisation. Then, as can be seen in Bangalore's software industry, industrialisation today has developed to the point that it now has the potential to bring great change to India's cities and regions as well to a regional structure across the nation.

Mainly in the field of economics, a relatively large number of research studies are already investigating this string of economic liberalisation policies and recent economic growth. Until now, however, both inside and outside India, the results of these studies do not sufficiently explain how industrialisation and industrial estates develop on a regional scale, and in how this reshapes India's regional structure on the local, regional and national levels. For a nation such as India, with plentiful land, rich regional variety and thought, but facing infrastructure

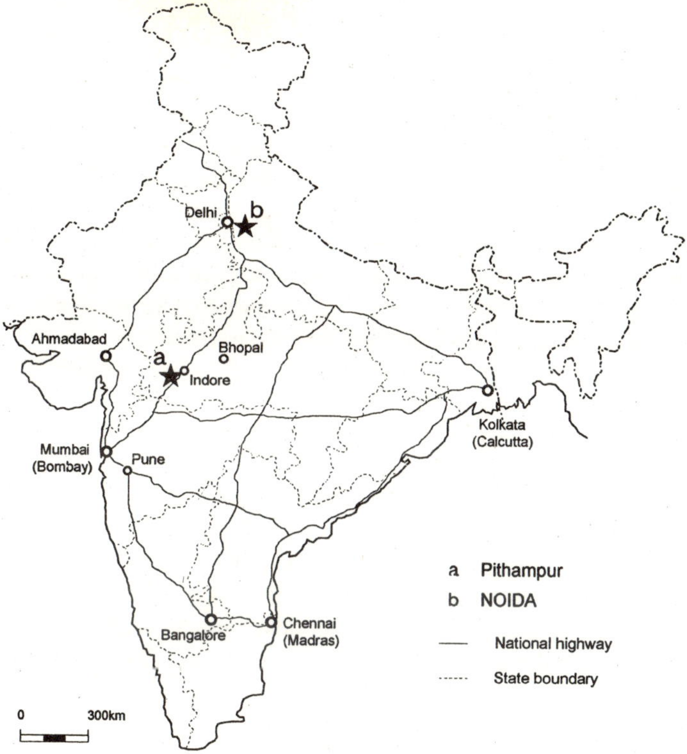

Figure 1.1: Location of study areas

RESEARCH METHOD

Because the main focus of this research is local scale studies such as industrial estate, village and urban regions, in addition to gathering statistics and materials from municipal offices and related organisations, we emphasised field work methods. Specifically, individual interviews comprised the majority of the research. Companies and labourers were targeted, as well as residential estate dwellers, shop owners, and residents of rural communities. Also, for the residential estate and rural community field studies, so that group members could share awareness of the issues, all members were interviewed together as a group. Especially in a study of sample villages adjacent to industrial estates, census-type studies to cover all households were performed.

ORGANISATION OF CHAPTERS

This book consists of four parts. Part I discusses the theoretical meaning and the role of industrial estates for regional development.

Part II looks at India overall from the perspective of advancement of industrialisation and distribution of industrial regions. Described in detail is the development process of the leading industries—especially the automobile and software industries—and the regional structure across the nation. For a nation like India with great amounts of land and with policies varying greatly from state to state, it is necessary to hold this macro-scaled investigation before considering micro-scale examples.

Parts III and IV, we look at the current state of two large-scale Indian industrial estate developments.

In Part III, Pithampur Industrial Growth Centre in MP State is taken as an example for a backward area. After discussing state policies and looking at the development process of Pithampur Industrial Growth Centre and the state of infrastructure, we consider the essential qualities of industries at Pithampur and the characteristics of the labour markets they have created. Additionally, residential estates and commercial areas are discussed in considering the urban development aspect of industrial estates. For neighbouring rural communities, the effects of industrialisation are highlighted mainly from the aspect of employment make-up and agricultural production.

In Part IV, NOIDA is highlighted as an example from a developed area. This section is organised in the same pattern as Part II except that there are no analyses of industrial labour markets and infrastructure conditions.

Finally, in the Conclusion, through a comparison of these two industrial estates, characteristics of industrial estate development in India are summarised. We look at these Indian qualities from an international perspective, also making comparisons and observations with SouthEast Asia and Japan.

PART I

INDUSTRIAL ESTATES AND REGIONAL DEVELOPMENTS

CHAPTER 2

Significance and Role of Industrial Estate Development: Research Framework

HIDENORI OKAHASHI

INDUSTRIAL ESTATE DEVELOPMENT: SIGNIFICANCE

The term industrial estate refers to a district which has undergone land development and received improvements in infrastructure according to a broad, comprehensive plan for the purpose of being shared by many corporations, and furthermore regularly zoned and subdivided. After World War II, this kind of industrial estate development was employed by countries around the world as a tool to advance industrialisation. Industrial estates play roles in both industrialisation and regional development. Development of special industrial areas, dispersal of industry away from city areas, and development of suburban areas are signs of regional development. In both India and Japan, industrial estate development has always been a powerful tool to advance regional development because of the transformations it brings forth. Additionally, when considered at the level of the region where it is performed, industrial development is closely related to urban and regional development in that this includes improved infrastructure, urbanisation, and formation of built-up areas. There, as typically seen in southeast Asia, industrialisation drives urban growth, and also has an effect on urban structure, validating this close relationship. In addition to advancing industrialisation, industrial estates help establish metropolitan areas by creating new industrial agglomerations, forming suburban spaces, and reshaping neighbouring regions. Through regional disparity issues, they also play a role in changing spacial structure across the nation.

INDUSTRIAL ESTATE DEVELOPMENT: ROLE

There are broadly tbree roles expected of industrial estate development: (1) improvement of locational conditions through targeted improvements in infrastructure (roads, electricity, water, housing, communications;

(2) creation of profits of agglomeration (business to business trade, external economies); (3) development to realise balanced growth between regions.

Regarding the first point, until now, the poor state of infrastructure such as roads, communication, ports and electricity have been strongly suspected as factors hindering India's industrialisation. It goes without saying that a considerable amount of time will be needed to resolve these infrastructure problems, and for this reason the establishment of industrial estates that make high demands on infrastructure availability should have a positive effect.[1] The role of IIPs is thought to be especially important as they are widely developed areas which contain not only industrial areas but also provide residential and commercial spaces; in addition to basic infrastructure such as electricity, water and communications, they also provide social infrastructure such as schools, hospitals and sewage.

Regarding the second point, when specific industry types are agglomerated in industrial estates, production complexes with close intercompany trade begin to form, making it possible to enjoy the benefits of various kinds of external economies. For industries such as automobile which rely on wide scale joint manufacturing of components, or the software industry, which requires special office services and infrastructure, the benefits are immence. The existence of industrial estates with these qualities in India has already been cited by Cadene and Holmstroem.[2] Certainly these types of industrial accumulations sometimes form spontaneously without industrial estate development, but construction of industrial estates for the purpose of forming industry agglomerations is also being strongly promoted.

Regarding the third point, to attain the goal of balanced growth, from the 1970s India has followed an industry decentralisation policies. Incentives have been granted to locate industries in backward areas or districts with no industries, but it were the industrial estates that realised this as a formal method. In India industrial estates have been emphasised as a method to achieve these regional policies.

RESEARCH FRAMEWORK

Not many academic works have considered industrial estate development in India. However, the findings of Haque,[3] who broadly investigated the state of industrial estates in the National Capital Region (NCR) are valuable. Haque does not simply summarise the current state of affairs, but cites several concerns that should be resolved for the future. The findings of CII[4] are not based on fieldwork for a specific region, but they are important because they reveal in theoretical terms the problems and potential of India's industrial estate development as related to industrial progress. From this, we can clearly see why governments and economic organisations are increasingly showing interest in industrial estates.

However, there is hardly any existing research which focuses on a specific industrial estate and considers in a detailed, multifaceted manner the state of regional change accompanying this development. DuPont[5] looks at the dynamics of change for a specific district, but focuses on migration, the labour market and employment conditions. The present book considers industrial estates more comprehensively than these previous studies. Since economic liberalisation, the influence of industrial estates in the sphere of industrialisation, urbanisation and regional development has increased. From a geographical perspective, perhaps what is needed is a scrupulous investigation of the real regional conditions and the multifaceted impact on surrounding regions, and to look at the future of India's land development.

To this end, in this book, research is performed in the areas of (1) industrial estate development, (2) urban development, and (3) rural development (see Figure 3.1). The first is the core of this study, and

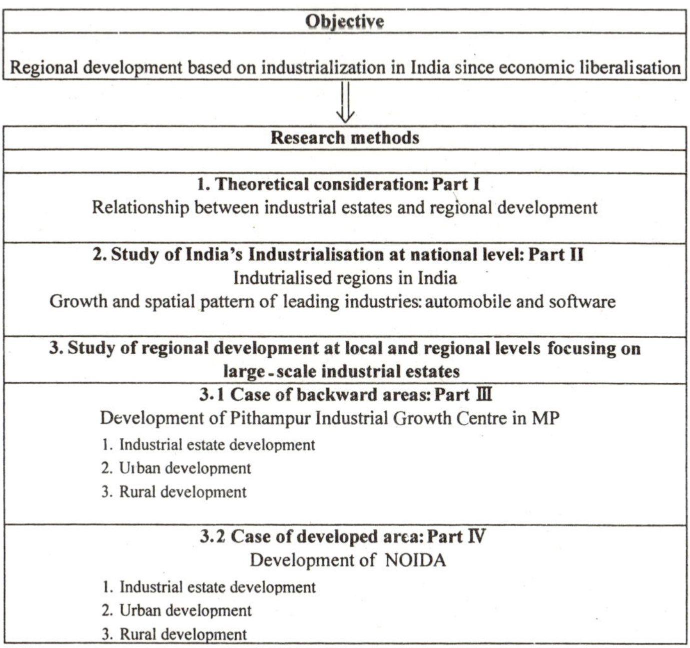

Figure 3.1: Research framework

reveals the quality of industrial estates as economic spaces. We especially focus on the development policies and planning of industrial estates, infrastructure conditions, industrial agglomeration and production structure, and structure of the industrial labour market. Under the second category, we investigate the urban space aspect of industrial estates. With the advance of industrialisation, housing development, and locations of commercial facilities and public facilities, IIPs form downtown and central areas, taking on the character of a city. For this urban space aspect, here we focus on the provision of housing for factory workers and establishment of residential estates, and further consider the growth of residential areas within the industrial estate area and growth of central areas. Under the third area of research, we investigate the impact of industrialisation on the neighbouring villages. In other words, we consider how development of industrial estates has affected agriculture, farmers, and village society itself. Especially important here is the link with the labour market and agricultural products market. Finally, by analysing the research findings, we reveal the regional formation caused by industrial estate development and its qualities.

NOTES

1 The Expert Group on the Commercialisation of Infrastructure Projects (Ministry of Finance), *The India Infrastructure Report*, New Delhi: J.M. Jain & Bros, 1997, p. 401.

2 P. Cadene and M. Holmstroem (eds.), *Decentralized Production in India: Industrial Districts, Flexible Specialization, and Employment*, New Delhi: Sage Publications, 1998.

3 M.S. Haque, *Industrial Estates in India: Organization, Structure and Role*, Delhi: Gyan Sagar Publications, 1999.

4 CII, *Report on Industrial Parks: Catalysts for State Level Industrialisation*, CII, 1998.

5 V. DuPont, *Decentralized Industrialization and Urban Dynamics: The Case of Jetpur in West India*, New Delhi: Sage Publications, 1995.

CHAPTER 3

Industrial Estate Development and Regional Policy: India and Japan

HIDENORI OKAHASHI

INDUSTRIAL ESTATE DEVELOPMENT IN INDIA

After independence, under the leadership of Prime Minister Nehru, India chose the socialist planned economy and opted for economic growth based on government-led mixed economic policies. It built the public sector around key industries by imposing economic controls on private industry through licensing system, and through import restrictions and restrictions on foreign direct investment. India aimed to achieve its growth goals by developing industry as a substitute for imports. Furthermore, her economic development objectives were extremely multifaceted. Along with industrial growth agricultural growth was also emphasised, and industrial development itself needed to take into consideration restricted concentration of economic power, protection of small-scale industry, and balanced growth between regions.

However, from the time of independence to the mid-1960s, there was no real regional policy that directly attempted to address the problem of disparity between regions or resolving regional problems. The Third Five Year Plan (1961-6) was a turning point, as this kind of conditional policy began to be enacted from the late 1960s. The process of this change is discussed below.[1]

One of the main plan objectives of the third plan was to achieve balanced regional growth. Urban growth issues began to be recognised as policy issues, and industry decentralisation began to be earnestly considered as a policy goal. For instance, the industrial estates created since 1956 were limited to small-scale industries, but from the 1960s the number of estates increased dramatically, and most of these were built not around urban but in rural areas. Also, in 1960s the first committees on industry decentralisation were established, and in 1969 two groups advised the government: Pande's working group, which looked at the determination of backwards areas, and Wanchoo's working group, which considered fiscal monetary policy to encourage the setting up of industries in backward areas.

Based on their recommendations, in the Fourth Five Year Plan (1969-74), the central government declared 229 districts as industrially backward, and began to enact concrete industry decentralisation policies for setting up industries in these backward regions. The policies provided such benefits as investment subsidies, favourable tax treatment, or low interest rate loans. Additionally, to further encourage investments in industry in backward areas, state governments also declared backward regions and provided preferential treatments in addition to the assistance from the central government.

In the Fifth Five Year Plan (1974-9), there was emphasis on protection and development of small-scale industries, and as promotional centres, District Industry Centres were set up to unify an administrative window. Another factor that served to further drive industry decentralisation was a clause in the industry investment allowance policy that prohibited corporations from establishing or expanding sites and offices in urban areas with 5,00,000 or more people, and in standard urban areas with 1 million or more people.

From the 1980s, a 'no-industry district' (districts with no large or medium size industries) category was added to the industry investment allowance policy, and these areas were promoted over backward areas as preferred sites for development. For the 83 no-industry districts nationwide, extremely favourable investment allowances and infrastructure improvements were offered. In 1983, in addition to the existing backward areas, three additional categories, A, B, and C were added, and depending on the category different levels of subsidies or loans were made available.

Pithampur Industrial Growth Centre (to be discussed later) is typical of industrial estates from this era, and its location in the no-industry district of Dhar most likely afforded to newly located factories extremely favourable subsidy, loan and infrastructure conditions. Moreover, from the 1980s, restrictions on investment and site location were also eased.

In 1988, the central government itself began to get involved in industrial estate development. It announced a plan to build 100 industrial growth centres nationwide in less than five years, and named 70 growth centres for the first phase. Investments in electricity, water, communications and infrastructure improvements were made (between Rs. 25-

30 million per centre). The goal was to attract corporations to these backward areas. Soon the plan ballooned into a grandiose plan to build growth centres in all 430 or so districts.

In contrast to this industrial estate development which intended to correct regional disparities, for the software industry, which began expanding rapidly after economic liberalisation, software technology parks (STPs) began to be developed in a handful of cities. This clearly shows that the economic liberalisation that allowed the influx of overseas investment to grow, new policy was required that would deal with India's industrial estate development in ways different than up to now.

Why are industrial estates important for foreign companies? Kawabata and Ishizutsu[2] argue that when companies especially Japanese firms, build factories in Asia, various problems arise. In a foreign country where the language is not understood and where industrial infrastructure is weak, even considering the settting up of a new factory, poses problems, such as how to find a site and build the factory, how to secure electricity, water and labour force, how to transport raw materials and products, and where to the staff live. Locating the factory in an industrial estate provides solution to many of these problems.

PROBLEMS IN INDUSTRIAL ESTATE DEVELOPMENT: JAPAN-INDIA COMPARISON

Among the many problems cited in India's industrial estate development,[3] most serious are:

(1) There is great disparity in the occupancy rates of different industrial estates. This is because industrial estate marketing has not been emphasised on and many have been developed in areas where there was no demand.

(2) The level of infrastructure and provision of basic services and amenities is insufficient.

(3) As can be seen in the state of roads and drainages, maintenance of the estate after completion is poor. One reason for this is the State Industrial Development Corporations (SIDCs), which run the estates, have not sufficiently arranged for infrastructure maintenance and services. Another related factor is that infrastructure for remaining settlements are not improved.

(4) The SIDC is not emphasising administrative issues after selling the lots. In other words, no comprehensive industrial estate development plan has been put into place.

(5) The SIDC provides almost no support operations to incoming companies. To deal with these problems, in some cases such as NOIDA and Greater NOIDA which are discussed in this book, a comprehensive development organisation has been set up to address these issues. In these cases some of the abovementioned problems can be resolved.

These points summarise the issues seen in industrial estate development in India, but what problems are seen in Japan? Let us make a comparison. Problems 2 and 3 are not regarded as important in Japan, which has higher infrastructure standards. On the other hand, problems 1, 4 and 5 apply even to Japan. This is related to the fact that industrial estate development in India is mainly handled by the states and in Japan by local governments, both of which are public bodies.

Kawabata[4] proposes including Japan's industrial estate development in a broad-viewed industrial policy. Municipalities perform much of the development in Japan which frequently leads to finances being the primary concern, and a narrow perspective. In India, on the other hand, the states are the basic developing entity, and until economic liberalisation, the government held strong control over site regulation through industry allowances, allowing it to develop a broad perspective sooner than Japan, and contributing to better correction of regional disparities. This aspect can be seen in the two industrial estates covered in this book.

Furthermore Kawabata[5] cites the necessity in Japan for industrial estates to be featured in the independent industrial strategy or global strategy of regions. Until now, in both India and Japan, entrants to industrial estates were largely domestic corporations, and this led to the weakness of the global strategy. The difficulty of easily finding about industrial estate data for the nation as a whole is also probably related to this point.

In both Japan and India, there is plenty of evidence to support Kawabata's suggestion[6] that the policy emphasis should move from factory concentration to industrial agglomeration, from 'real estate business' to 'industrial estate management'. Of India's industrial estates, the fact that we should be looking at industrial agglomeration like NOIDA lends credibility to this perspective. Also, 'industrial estate management' overlaps with problems 4 and 5 previously discussed. Here, we would like to point out that in private industrial estate development in southeast Asia, there are already examples to support this.

A comparison of Indian industrial estates to southeast Asian countries should contribute to resolving these problems in future.

(1) In India, it is mostly domestic corporations that are located in industrial estates, but in southeast Asia overwhelmingly foreign corporations.
(2) In India industrial estates are used as a tool to correct regional disparity. This perspective also exists in southeast Asia, but the priority is economic growth.
(3) Construction of industrial estates in India has been entirely left to the public sector, but in South-East Asia, private corporations such as Japanese general trading companies have also set up industrial estates.
(4) In India, construction and administration of industrial estates is done at the state level, but in Thailand, the developing organisation is usually under the jurisdiction of the central government.

As can be seen from this in comparison of industrial estates in the three regions of India, southeast Asia and Japan should be an interesting research area for the future.

NOTES

1 This portion is based on the following literatures: S. Nakayama, K. Fujiwara and K. Kitagawa, 'Indo no Chiikiseisaku no Tenkai to Mondai (Regional Development Policies in India: Problems and Prospects)', *Annals of the Association of Economic Geographers,* vol. 25, 1979, pp. 149-64; M. Koga, 'Indo ni okeru Chiikiseisaku no Tenkai (Development of Regional Policies in India)', in T. Kawashima and I. Kamozawa (eds.), *Gendai sekai no chiiki seisaku (Regional Policies in Contemporary World)*, Tokyo: Taimeido,1988, pp. 162-89; K. Inoue, *Industrial Development Policy of India*,Tokyo: Institute of Developing Economics, 1992; G. Singh, *Industrial Incentives and Subsidies*, New Delhi: Deep & Deep Publications, 1994.

2 M. Kawabata and S. Ishizutsu, 'Ajia no Kogyodanchi to Nikkei Sogoshosha no Kaihatsu Shuhou (Industrial Estates in Asia and Development Method of Japan's General Trading Companies)', in M. Kawabata and M. Miyanaga (eds.), *Daikyousou Jidai no 'Monozukuri' Kyoten-Kougyodanchi no Sabaibaru Senryaku (Manufacturing Clusters under Mega-Competition: Survival Strategies of Industrial Estates)*, Tokyo: Shinhyoron, 1998, pp. 174-94.

3 CII pointed out this problem: *Report on Industrial Parks: Catalysts for State Level Industrialisation*, CII, 1998.

4 M. Kawabata, 'Kougyoudanchi no Genkyo to Sore wo Torimaku Kankyo (Present Situation and Circumstances of Industrial Estates)', in M. Kawabata and M. Miyanaga (eds.), *Daikyousou Jidai no 'Monozukuri' Kyoten-Kougyodanchi no Sabaibaru Senryaku (Manufacturing Clusters under Mega-Competition: Survival Strategies of Industrial Estates)*, Tokyo: Shinhyoron, 1998, pp. 16-40.

5 M. Kawabata, 'Daikyosou Jidai no "Monozukuri" Kyoten wo Mezashite (Aiming at Manufacturing Clusters under Mega-Competition)', in M. Kawabata and M. Miyanaga (eds.), *Daikyousou Jidai no "Monozukuri" Kyoten-Kougyodanchi no Sabaibaru Senryaku (Manufacturing Clusters under Mega-Competition: Survival Strategies of Industrial Estates)*, Tokyo: Shinhyoron, 1998, p. 225.

6 Ibid., p. 228.

PART II

NEW DEVELOPMENTS IN INDIA'S INDUSTRIALISATION

CHAPTER 4

India's Industrialisation and Industrialised Regions

HIDENORI OKAHASHI

INDUSTRIAL STRUCTURE OF INDIA

Like other developing nations, India's industrial structure at the time of independence was overwhelmingly centred on the agricultural sector. In terms of GDP, in 1950 agriculture comprised 57 per cent of GDP while the manufacturing sector's share was less than 15 per cent. However, agriculture's share of GDP steadily shrank with a transition to growth in the industrial sector, transportation and communications. In 1999, the agricultural sector's share fell below 30 per cent for the first time, standing at 29 per cent, and the industrial sector increased its share to 25 per cent. However, agriculture's share of GDP was still greater than the manufacturing industry's, and the industrial sector percentage was lower than in the ASEAN countries.

In nominal GDP terms the economic scale of India still exceeds that of all ASEAN countries. Its ability to enable its industries to grow by substituting domestic goods for imports is a proof of its economic size and the economy of its domestic market. But on the other hand, its reliance on trade (ratio of total commerce to GDP) is extremely small, and the economy still has characteristics of a closed economy.

Although international trade is deficit-based in nature, with imports in chronic excess of exports, the ratio of exported products occupied by industrial products in 1960 was 45 per cent, and has increased to the current level of 80 per cent, showing that industry has taken centre stage in terms of exports. Since 1992, exports has been increasing dramatically. However, textiles and handcrafted products (particularly processed diamond products) account for over half the industrially manufactured products while machinery and mechanical devices account for less than 20 per cent. This is because of the international competition in durable consumer goods industries.

CHARACTERISTICS OF INDUSTRIALISATION IN INDIA

Industrialisation in post-independence has been through import substitution, beginning with government-run heavy chemical industries, and diversification of textiles into aircraft and petrochemicals. This has led to industrial structure of high standard. 'Made in India', now means broad technological prowess. At the same time, however, this industrialisation has also brought the problems of a high cost economy. The industrial environment has been undergoing change since economic liberalisation in 1991. The introduction of foreign capital has especially intensified competition in the market.

This is because since shifting to an open economy, foreign firms, attracted by the size of the Indian market, all jumped in at the same time. The growth of consumer durables such as home appliances has been dizzying, and the world leading automobile manufacturers have entered the Indian market. Before economic liberalisation, there was no competition because each product market was dominated by one or two companies. The domestic market was a seller's market, and improvements in product quality were hardly ever seen. For instance, until the arrival of foreign capital in the mid-1980s, India's domestic automobiles had not undergone a model change in nearly 40 years.

This product supply environment had the effect of restricting domestic consumption demand. From the late 1980s, with a growth in product offerings and improrement in quality, the consumer market showed rapid growth and a consumption boom ensued. Bicycles, wristwatches, and transistor radios expanded to all income levels, and so much so that today colour televisions, refrigerators and scooters are the Indian version of 'the three sacred treasures'.

Until this time, mention of the word 'India' elicited images of a polarised society of the poor masses and the rich elite. Even for data of consumption classes, it is true that 60 per cent of all households are categorised as falling below the poverty line. However, the middle class has grown to 36.3 per cent. This market of 300 million people belonging to the middle class or higher is the target of foreign capital in the post-economic liberalisation era.

However, the largest subset of this middle class is the lower middle class (comprising approximately 60 per cent of the entire middle class), and even in the capital and major cities its yearly income is only Rs. 48,000-120,000. When considering the market prices of consumer goods, members of this class just might be able to afford a colour television, but a scooter or a passenger car is simply out of their reach. Therefore, the class which can purchase these high-priced items is the roughly 60 million people, or 14 million households of the affluent and the upper middle class. Companies are forced to compete for this narrow market. The automobile industry in India today is currently facing this dilemma.

ECONOMIC REGIONAL STRUCTURE AND INDUSTRIALISED REGIONS

India's economy can be divided into four regions of east, west, north and south. The east region centred around West Bengal includes Kolkata, the former capital of British India that became industrialised early on. Even after independence, the heavy industry was concentrated in the eastern represented by the steel industries in Jamshedpur-Rourkela created based on hydro-power resources, coal from the Damodar catchment, and rich iron ore deposits. However, with the decline of the jute industry and difficulty in expanding heavy and chemical industries, industrialisation in the east has stagnated.

On the other hand, in addition to the cotton industry from the colonial days, machine and petrochemical industries, and comprehensive industrial districts are being formed in Gujarat and Maharashtra states in the west. India's commercial and financial capital Mumbai is a significant concentration of the durable goods industry such as home appliances and bicycles, as well as the software industry.

With a third of the overall population residing in the northern region, grain production is centred around the Indus River tributaries and the Ganga and even by Indian standards, the population in this region is dense. Industrialisation had lagged behind, but in recent years, the national capital region of Delhi has emerged as a large industrial centre.

The southern region had been the centre of agricultural activity mainly through plantations, but since independence, advancements have been made in heavy and chemical industries. In Bangalore, also called India's Silicon Valley, advanced industries such as airplane manufacturing, machine tooling, and software have developed. And south India's largest commercial city of Chennai has produced goods ranging from cotton to cars, and software.

Thus a transformation is occurring in its industrialisation pattern where the west is in a position of advantage, the east is stagnating, and the north and the south are growing. In order to look with more closing at the regional economic structure of India, we rank each state according to its per capita income and ratio of manufacturing industry to overall state income.

First, states with high income levels include Delhi, Punjab, Haryana, Maharashtra and Gujarat. Of these, the industrialisation in Punjab and Haryana approximates the national average, and agriculture seems to play a large role in increasing income. On the other hand, industrialisation in Maharashtra and Gujarat are the highest nationally, and this is thought to be related to the high income level in these states. In contrast to these high income groups, Bihar, Orissa, UP, MP and Rajasthan are cited as states with lowest income. Industrialisation in these states is below the national average, and the ratio of population living below the poverty line is high, with Orissa at 44.7 per cent, Bihar at 40.8 per cent and MP at 36.7 per cent. Because these states are in the interior of India and belong to the Hindi speaking world they are called the Hindi Belt, and even in India are the regions most troubled by poverty.

In addition to the divisions of east, west, north and south, the disparity between inner regions and coastal regions is evident. Underdevelopment of inner regions is due to significant inequalities in regional industrial distribution. Most of the current primary industrial regions were formed in the British colonial period, and these have become concentrated in specific coastal cities such as Mumbai and Kolkata. At time of independence, up to 80 per cent of industrial labourers were concentrated in the coastal cities.

Even 20 years after independence in 1970, Maharashtra in the west and West Bengal in the east had significant advantages in industrial production. Even after enforcement of policies to correct regional differences, the disparity between coastal and inner regions remains basically unresolved. Significant here is the growing importances since 1970s of north India including Delhi, an inland city. At the same time, this signifies that disparities started to appear even within the Hindi Belt, between areas near Delhi and areas not near Delhi.

CHAPTER 5

Growth of the Automobile Industry

KAZUO TOMOZAWA

INTRODUCTION

India's automotive industry is representative of the recent economic growth in that country. India's automobile production in 2003 was 1.16 million vehicles. Compared to the 3,70,000 vehicles produced in 1993, in 10 years the industry's capacity has more than tripled in size (see Figure 5.1). India has joined Japan, Korea and China as a major auto manufacturer producing more than 1 million vehicles per year in Asia, taking the first step to becoming a major automobile nation.

This growth of the automotive industry since the 1990s is closely related to the expansion of the middle class. Since the implementation of liberalisation policies in India, foreign investment has been active in all

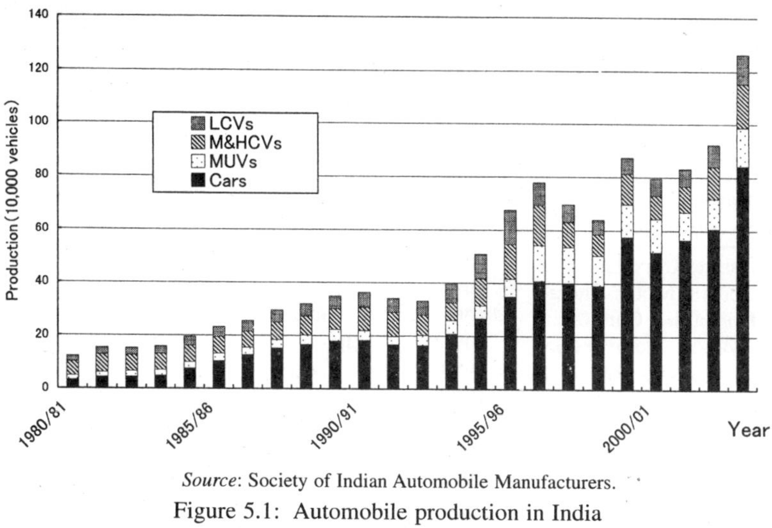

Source: Society of Indian Automobile Manufacturers.

Figure 5.1: Automobile production in India

sectors of industry, bringing increases in business and employment as well as income. This has brought about the growth of the working middle class and expansion of consumption, leading to even more foreign investment. Led by this economic growth circuit, India's automobile industry has also grown steadily.

The aim of this chapter is to understand the growth process of and locational trends for this rapidly growing industry, and to reveal its market characteristics.

THE AUTOMOBILE INDUSTRY UNDER ECONOMIC CONTROLS (PRE-1970s)

Compared to other Asian countries, India's automotive industry has a relatively long history (see Table 5.1). Hindustan Motors in 1942 and Premier Automobiles in 1944 were founded with local capital. Other four-wheel vehicles companies such as TELCO, Ashok Leyland, Mahindra & Mahindra (M&M), and two-wheeler vehicles companies such as Escorts and Bajaj Auto were founded in rapid succession. This

Table 5.1: Outline of automobile companies in Inida

Company	*Foundation*	*Turnover** (*Rs. in million*)	*Employees** (*in number*)	*Location***
Hindustan Motors	1942	10,747	7,924	Chennai
Mahindra & Mahindra	1945	45,968	11,800	Mumbai
Tata Motors (TELCO)	1945	108,551	22,254	Mumbai
Ashok Leyland	1948	30,740	11,860	Chennai
Bajaj Tempo	1958	8,544	7,153	Pune
Eicher Motors	1959	5,326	925	Delhi
Maruti Udyog	1981	90,636	4,590	Delhi
Swaraj Mazda	1983	3,724	748	Chandigarh
DaimlerChrysler India	1994	2,888	353	Pune
General Motors India	1994	1,706	544	Gurgaon
Honda Siel Cars India	1995	9,854	795	Noida
Hyundai Motor India	1996	40,602	2,677	Chennai
Toyota Kirloskar Motor	1997	17,696	2,050	Bangalore
Volvo India	1997	2,810	360	Bangalore
Fiat India	1997	8,909	1,915	Mumbai
Ford India	1999	10,514	n.a.	Chennai
SkodaAuto India	1999	3,836	123	Aurangabad

Notes: * 2003 fiscal year, ** location of main office.
Source: Society of Indian Automobile Manufacturers.

era could be called the groundbreaking years for India's automotive industry.

After India gained independence in 1947, the government implemented economic policies to establish a socialist production system, and for a long time, the automotive industry was also subjected to the regulation and control of the government. This dates back to the 'Industrial Policy Resolution' of 1948, which classified the automobile industry as an industry of importance that would be controlled and regulated by the government. Also, the industry fell under jurisdiction of the 'Industries (Development and Regulation)'. Act of 1951 which made it compulsory to acquire licences for manufacturing products. This had the effect of protecting the profits of existing companies, while at the same time greatly restricting vehicle design and expansion of automakers into new businesses. Overall, these policies worked to protect the domestic industry, and in the 1950s it was impossible for a foreign corporation to build automobiles in India. Later, with high tariffs slapped on imported automobiles and imported automobile parts, it became extremely difficult even to import assembled vehicles. Supported by these economic policies, India achieved 100 per cent domestic vehicle production in the late 1960s.

In the period between independence and the late 1970s, the growth of the automobile industry was characteristic of the period of economic controls. While domestic markets were shielded from competition through protective policies, these policies became barriers that hindered vehicle production and improvement by eliminating competition, and slowed the pace of technology. This could be seen in the weakness of four wheeler production after the oil shock. Passenger vehicle production, increased from 30,000 vehicles in 1964 to 40,000 vehicles in 1973, but fell to 29,000 vehicles in 1979. The direct cause for the drop in production was the increase in production costs and stagnant demand caused by the oil shock, but these causes were essentially rooted in structural issues which extended to all areas of Indian industry. The greatest factor was a shift to 'high cost' industrial production due to poor infrastructure, small-scale manufacturing, low factory utilisation, and decreasing labour productivity. For the automotive industry which grew due to government protection in the 1960s, the oil shock of the 1970s caused the underlying barriers to surface, and this brought on the loss of competitive ability.

THE AUTOMOBILE INDUSTRY UNDER PARTIAL ECONOMIC LIBERALISATION (1980s)

To improve this high-cost economy, upon coming to power in 1980 Prime Minister Indira Gandhi launched new policies to improve the efficiencies of various industry sectors. Their main impact was relaxation of the licensing controls. This made it possible to expand productivity and invest in modernisation. Gradually the government began to allow capital investment and technical implementation by foreign companies. Through the changes brought on by these economic policies, India's economy began its journey to economic liberalisation.

It was in this period that passenger vehicle production increased. Until the 1970s, the passenger vehicle market was controlled by two companies—Hindustan Motors and Premier Automobiles. While production for both companies remained flat through the 1980s, Maruti Udyog, formed through a Japan-India joint venture to produce a small car, gained explosive popularity with its mainstay vehicle, the 800cc Maruti, and by 1989 had captured approximately 60 per cent of the market share.

In the heavy and medium commercial vehicle sector, no large changes were seen in levels of production, and the market was controlled by two privately funded companies—TELCO with 70 per cent share and Ashok Leyland with 30 per cent share. The light commercial vehicle market, saw a gradual increase. In addition to the Japanese companies Toyota, Nissan, Mitsubishi and Mazda, in 1985 TELCO joined the fray, and competition between these companies intensified. Because India had bad roads, and illegal oversized loads were frequently transported over long distances, light commercial vehicles from Japanese joint ventures were seen as being insufficiently durable. For this reason they were unable to gain market share like they had done in the passenger vehicle segment.

With the growth in competitors and vehicle production, the 1980s can be viewed as the take-off period for India's automotive industry. Also, this period is notable for the entry of Japanese automakers. Apart from the four-wheel vehicle segment mentioned above, Honda, Suzuki, and Yamaha entered into joint ventures with Indian partners to produce two-wheel motorised vehicles and played an important role in enlarging this segment.

THE AUTOMOBILE INDUSTRY DURING THE LIBERALISATION PERIOD (POST-1990s)

In the early 1990s, following the assassination of Prime Minister Rajiv Gandhi, the Indian government was thrown into disorder. It also faced its worst economic crisis since gaining independence, caused by chronic budget deficits. Unable to escape the effects of the political and economic crises, the automobile industry saw decreased production volumes in 1992 and 1993 due to a slump in demand. Noteworthy during this period of stagnant growth was the departure of Japanese companies from the light commercial vehicle segment. As mentioned above, market competition was fiercest in here, productivity of Japanese joint ventures was low and they were faced with slow growth in production volume. Political and economic instability added to the concerns, and Japanese corporations exited the segment by dissolving the tie-ups or selling off their operations.

However, this economic crisis was short lived due to the stabilisation brought about by the Narasimha Rao administration's 'New Economic Policy'. The policy aimed to stabilise and fully liberalise the economy. Together with the recovery of the macro economy, the automotive industry underwent a second period of growth from the mid-1990s. This period is noteworthy for the arrival of international automakers and intensified competition in the passenger vehicle market. Here, we detail the movement of the companies established with foreign capital.

First, we look at the trends for Korean companies. In 1994, Daewoo Motor purchased management rights for DCM Toyota, a light commercial vehicle manufacturer. Changing the name to DCM Daewoo, it began production of a 1,500cc passenger vehicle in 1995. The company's strategy was to beat western and Japanese manufacturers to the midsize market, and prop up its low brand image by being a market pioneer. Then, it took aggressive steps, increasing its stock holdings to 92 per cent, taking control of the management, and introducing an 800cc compact car to directly compete with the Maruti 800. To attain the objective of quick growth in productivity, these operations required massive investments in a short period of time, and because a lot of parts had to be imported from Korea, there was the ever-present financial instability from the weakening rupee. Following the bankruptcy of the parent company Daewoo Motor in Korea in 2000, production was halted.

In 1998, Hyundai Motor established a 100 per cent funded production subsidiary (Hyundai India), and began to produce and sell two passenger vehicles, the Santro (1,000cc) and the Accent (1,300-1,500cc). Compared to Daewoo Motor, Hyundai's investments were more cautious, and initially production line equipment was brought in from its Canadian factory. Additional investment in Accent production was only committed after sales figures for the Santro line could be estimated. Additionally, emphasis was made on acquiring parts domestically, and when manufacturing began, 70 per cent of the parts were obtained locally. The sales of both vehicles were in synch with the sales of Maruti Udyog for the same vehicle classes. For Korean automakers, Hyundai's success stood in contrast to Daewoo's failure.

The growth of Japanese companies is also noteworthy. Honda, which had not ventured beyond the two-wheel sector until the early 1990s, through a joint venture with the Siel group established Honda Siel Cars India, and began production of the City (1,300cc-1,500cc) from 1997. The luxury model Accord was introduced in 2001. Growth was seen in the two-wheeler market as well. Hero Honda, a joint venture with the local Hero Group manufacturing motorcycles, opened a second factory in 1997—the world's largest motorcycle factory—and produced 1.6 million vehicles in 2003. In the scooter segment, Honda relinquished control of Kinetic Honda, established its own subsidiary (Honda Motorcycle and Scooter India) in Gurgaon, the suburbs of Delhi, and began supplying products in 2001. Toyota's Indian operations are behind the curve compared to other companies. In 1997 Toyota founded Toyota Kirloskar Motor together with Kirloskar, a medium-scale conglomerate, and began manufacture and sale of the Qualis, a utility vehicle, in 1999, and the Corolla in 2002.

From the United States, Ford and GM entered the market. Using an existing Mahindra & Mahindra factory known for producing Jeeps, Ford began production of the Escort (1,300cc) in 1996. In 1999 it established Ford India and began manufacturing the Ikon (1,600cc). Using a Hindustan Motors plant in the Vadodara suburbs, GM began producing the Astra (1,600cc). However, growth of market share for these two companies with no vehicle targeting the compact/low price car segment which is the core of the Indian market, can only be predicted for the short term.

Entrants can also be seen from Europe. DaimlerChrysler established a local subsidiary in 1995 and began assembling and selling India's first luxury car (E Class). Also, through its Skoda subsidiary, Volkswagen established a domestic corporation to manufacture passenger cars. Italy's Fiat, through the acquisition of Premier Automobiles' operations, is manufacturing compact passenger cars. Sweden's Volvo established Volvo India, and was the first foreign competitor to enter into the large commercial vehicle segment.

AUTOMOBILE FACTORY SITES

From around the time of independence to the 1960s, the automobile industry developed around Delhi, Mumbai (Bombay), Pune, Kolkata (Calcutta) and Chennai (Madras). Component manufacturers also located their sites around these cities. Figure 5.2 shows the locations of corporations (about 400) belonging to the Automotive Component Manufacturers Association of India (ACMA) for each company: starting year of production, the period of pre-1980 economic regulation, partial liberalisation of the 1980s, and full liberalisation of the 1990s. As shown in the figure, by the 1970s about half of the component manufacturers had set up shop, but most of them were located in the above mentioned five cities, revealing clearly their status as agglomerations. The existence of these pre-existing agglomerations had a major effect on new automotive industry investment. This is because the production of automobiles requires many parts and components, and the cost of transporting these components cannot be ignored. Also, interstate commerce in India attracted a 4 per cent tax, and there were problems with road infrastructure and shipping which had to be overcome. To lower transportation costs and mitigate risks, it was advantageous to locate one's business in an existing agglomeration.

At the same time, however, in the 1980s, when partial liberalisation began to appear, new automotive plants were being developed far away from these industrial agglomerations. There were two types of sites: those which maintained a certain degree of proximity with existing agglomerations, and those which were completely isolated. Maruti Udyog's and Hero Honda's sites in the southwest suburbs of Delhi and DCM Toyota's foray into the eastern suburbs are examples of the first of these. Examples of the latter are the establishments of Eicher Mitsubishi (now Eicher Motors) and Kinetic Honda, and the branch plants of Hindustan Motors and Bajaj Tempo at Pithampur Industrial Growth Centre, which is situated in a backward region in Madhya Pradesh and discussed in Part III. To avoid the concentration of industries in large cities, the Indian government developed policies that encouraged selling up of new industrial sites in backward regions. Large-scale industrial estates were developed in by the backward regions, and sites were

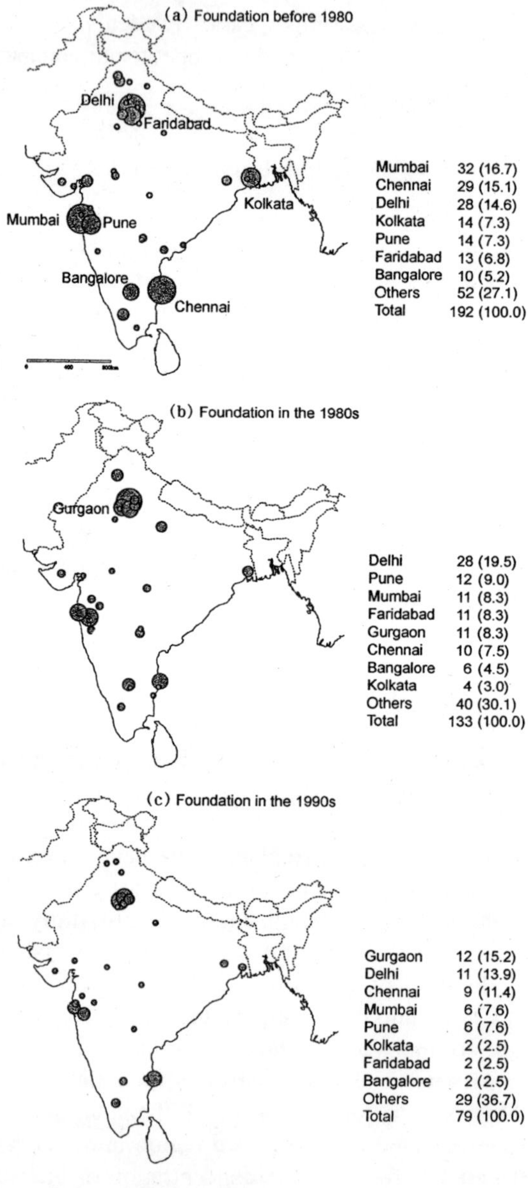

Note: Refer to ACMA members.
Source: ACMA *Buyers' Guide*, 2002.

Figure 5.2: Location of automobile component manufacturers

prohibited from being located in large cities (for example, a new factory had to be situated at least 25 km away from a city with more than 1 million people). As a result of new automobile factories were located in industrial estates developed in rural areas, which were created to correct regional differences. Furthermore, influenced by the sudden increase in production at Maruti Udyog, there was a trend for component manufacturers to concentrate in the Delhi metropolitan area, and 38 per cent of newly established companies in the 1980s settled here.

With full liberalisation in the 1990s, companies were able to select factory locations according to their will. In response, new investment in the 1990s was clearly targeted around existing automotive industrial agglomerations. In north India, investment has being made in the area surrounding Delhi. Representative of this is NOIDA, which is discussed in Part IV. Daewoo Motor and Honda have made investments here. Another location is Gurgaon, where in addition to Hero Honda's second factory and the creation of Honda Motorcycle & Scooter India, Suzuki is planning to go it alone in establishing a two-wheel vehicle company.

In south India, investment is tending toward the area surrounding Chennai. Ford India decided to enter into this region after evaluating the component manufacturer agglomeration, availability of a skilled labour force, state government incentives, stability of the ports and electricity supply. For similar reasons, Hyundai Motor has also established its subsidiary in the Chennai area. In a joint venture with Mitsubishi, Hindustan Motors located its new plant in this region to manufacture passenger vehicles. Also, Toyota Kirloskar Motor and Volvo India have begun operations in Bangalore. In west India, more than Mumbai, investments are being made inland at Pune (Daimler Chrysler India) and Aurangabad (Skoda).

Therefore, most passenger vehicle plants established after 1995 have been located in the Delhi, Chennai and Pune areas, and have secured locations near existing agglomerations. In Mumbai, however, partly due to the fall of Premier Automobiles, the automotive industry is stagnant. As the government of West Bengal has been communist controlled for a long time, and due to frequent problems with labour, Kolkata as a location to set up industry has had little appeal. Thus, bollowing economic liberalisation, India's automotive industry agglomerations are undergoing great change.

CHARACTERISTICS OF THE AUTOMOBILE MARKET

India's automobile market can be largely divided into the passenger vehicle segment and the commercial vehicle segment, which includes vehicles such as trucks and buses. Here, we discuss the market characteristics of the passenger vehicle segment which has undergone significant growth in recent years.

The passenger vehicle segment consists of three categories: A passenger cars, B utility vehicles, and C multipurpose vehicles. B includes recreational vehicles while vans belong to the C group. Passenger cars are further subdivided according to length: A1 (under 3.4 m), A2 (3.4-4.0 m), A3 (4.0-4.5 m), A4 (4.5-4.7 m), A5 (4.7-5.0 m), and A6 (over 5.0 m). Of course, longer vehicles are more expensive.

In 2002, the nationwide passenger vehicle sales stood at 7,08,000 vehicles; these 43 per cent were A2 vehicles. A2 consists mainly of 1,000cc displacement class vehicles made by four companies. A typical selling price is Rs. 3,50,000 (Re. 1 = ¥ 2.50 appx). About 20 per cent of passenger cars are A1, but the only car belonging to this category is Maruti Udyog's Maruti 800, which boasts of greatest sales volume for any single car model in India. It is also the most affordable car about Rs. 2,50,000. Eight companies fight in the A3 subcategory, which makes up 13 per cent of the passenger car market. It is both the segment with the most intense competition, and the market with the largest sales volume. Prices vary, but the average is Rs. 6,00,000. The A4-A6 classes can be called the India's luxury car segment; together they comprise only 1 per cent of the market. Value-added passenger vehicles belonging to B and C segment, and while being niche products account for 16 per cent and 7 per cent of the passenger vehicle market, respectively. We can conclude that India's passenger car market is centred around the compact and low-priced A1 and A2 categories, and A3 is the growth segment.

Sales volumes of each manufacturer are shown in Table 5.2. The average sales volume per car maker is 60,000 cars. In automobile manufacturing, a single factory needs to produce 1,00,000 vehicles per year to achieve economies of scale; on an average, India's automobile industry is not enjoying the merits of this scale (in India, sales volume and production volume are roughly equal). Also, only the top three companies are actually selling more than 1,00,000 vehicles per year; of the remaining nine companies, all but one are selling less than 50,000 vehicles per year. This small-scade of production and sales is a problem for India's automotive industry, and the further introduction of manu-

Table 5.2: Sales volumes of Indian passenger vehicles in 2002

Company	*Sales*	*(%)*	*Category*
Maruti Udyog	3,30,182	(46.6)	A1, A2, A3, B, C
Tata Motors	1,04,412	(14.7)	A2, A3, B
Hyundai Motor India	1,03,536	(14.6)	A2, A3, A5
Mahindra & Mahindra	52,287	(7.4)	B, C
Toyota Kirloskar Motor	30,299	(4.3)	A4, A5, B
Fiat India	25,936	(3.7)	A2, A3
Hindustan Motors	19,329	(2.7)	A3, A4, B
Ford India	15,406	(2.2)	A3, A5
Honda Siel Cars India	13,296	(1.9)	A3, A5
General Motors India	8,286	(1.2)	A3, A4
Bajaj Tempo	4,030	(0.6)	B
DaimlerChrysler India	1,109	(0.2)	A4, A5, A6
Total	7,08,108	(100.0)	

Source: Society of Indian Automobile Manufacturers.

facturers will make the competition even more intense.

Here we would like to look at distinguishing sales characteristics of the top three automakers. Maruti Udyog has the largest sales volume and commands 47 per cent share. Its strengths are total control over the A1 segment and the largest sales volume in the A2 segment. It maintains yearly production and sales volumes of over 3,30,000 vehicles, and is the only company in India which has been able to achieve economies of scale. Also, it has a network 280 of dealers covering all of India. In 2002, Suzuki obtained management control (until then the company was jointly managed with the Government of India), and under it's leadership, cost cutting and sales strengthening initiatives have been advanced. From these conditions, it appears that Maruti Udyog's leading position will not be challenged for some time.

India's number two automaker TELCO (now Tata Motors) is notable for increasing its sales volume in an industry which is generally challenging for a private company. TELCO specialised in medium and large commercial vehicles until the 1970s. It entered the small commercial vehicle market in the 1980s, and the passenger car segment in the 1990s. In addition to the largest sales volume for the small, medium and large commercial vehicle segments, it has also improved it sales numbers in the A2, A3, and B segments by introducing affordable, 100 per cent Indian-made passenger cars. It is distinctive in being able to independently develop products targeted at each segment of the automobile market.

The number three automaker Hyundai Motor India's achievements are the most astounding. While other foreign companies were targeting the A3 and higher segments, it found success in a market strategy that concentrated on the A2 segment. Its sales volume in the A2 market is a close second to Maruti Udyog's, and despite fiercest competition, it has succeeded in reaching the number one position in the A3 segment.

The characteristics shared by each company is that while focusing on a market where sales volume could be expected, they also sold vehicles for segments which were likely to experience growth.

SUMMARY

Due to estimated annual economic growth of 5-6 per cent and the resultant expansion of the middle class, and due to following changes improved access to loans in the financial sector, the automotive market is expected to grow in the future. For this reason, the world's leading automakers regard India together with China as the last and largest market. Every leading manufacturers is establishing his corporate presence, building production systems and developing sales networks. However, currently this is not a money-making market. For a market predicted to expand in the future, current moves by competitors are strategic ones designed to secure a large piece of the pie. Also, some companies are positioning their newly created overseas affiliates with a global strategy in mind, setting up production facilities to provide vehicles for the South Asia market.

However, this influx of companies into the Indian automotive market also signifies the beginning of a period of excess competition. Including companies in the utility vehicle and multipurpose segments, there are 17 automakers producing cars in India, more than in Japan. This is leading to concerns about fierce competition. Some companies have already been shaken out of the market. Companies achieving economies of scale are very few and low productivity will continue to be a problem.

From the perspective of site location, Japan-based foreign investment is concentrated in the Delhi metropolitan area, and the status of the area as a centre for automotive industry has improved. While Chennai and Pune have seen foreign investment and component manufacturers are located there, instability of main corporations and labour issues have affected the favourability of Mumbai and Kolkata as automotive industry. Also, cities such as Bangalore are gaining new automotive industry investments. In this way, foreign investment since the 1990s is repainting the old map of India's automotive industry.

CHAPTER 6

Growth of the Software Industry and Agglomeration in Large Cities

KENTARO KUWATSUKA AND HIROFUMI KITAGAWA

INDIA'S SOFTWARE INDUSTRY IN THE SPOTLIGHT

The term 'IT' has penetrated our lives to the point that it has become an everyday term. Its use is no longer restricted to the developed countries. Together with this change, the image of India as 'age old India' is also changing. This is not merely because Indian software engineers are making a wave in developed countries like the United States, and Japan, but also because large Indian cities like Bangalore are attracting worldwide attention as software industry centres. India's software industry growth, together with the growth in manufacturing industries such as automobiles, is a distinctive feature of India's post-liberalisation economy.

India's software companies have taken advantage of the labour cost and time zone differences between India and the developed countries to begin software development in India. Made possible through advances in information and communication technology, the Indian software story is an example of how to conquer distances on a global scale. However, the software industry is not one which can be located anywhere. From a geographical perspective, the software industry is concentrated in a few large cities, and is known for software engineers and corporations demanding proximity to each other in the software development process. This model can be compared to the Silicon Valley in the United States.

Paradoxically, while growing globally through advances in information and communication technology and crossing international borders, the software industry, known as the knowledge industry, also tends to be concentrated in large cities. In formation of regional structure, large cities play an important role. For this reason, to understand the regional structure in post-economic liberalisation India, it is also necessary to understand the regional growth pattern of India's software industry. In this chapter, we provide an overview of the growth process of the software industry in India, and characteristics of that regional growth.

Also, to understand the state of India's software industry, a database was created for our analyses using the *Indian Software and Service Directory 2002* as a basic resource. This industry blue book was published in 2002 by the National Association of Software and Service Companies (NASSCOM). As of December 2001, 854 software companies and related organisations were members of NASSCOM. The combined revenues of these member companies accounted for approximately 95 per cent of the total revenues of the software and service industry.[1] Macro-level statistics of India's software and service industry are compiled by NASSCOM; there are no sufficiently organised publications to provide insight into the industry on a regional scale. The data of NASSCOM though limited is nevertheless considered to be effective in observing regional growth of relevant industries.

SOFTWARE INDUSTRY TRENDS

First, we discuss the transformations India's software industry has undergone. The combined domestic and export revenue of Indian software and related services industries, was Rs. 24.7 billion in 1994. In 1998 this grew to Rs. 167.5 billion, and in 2002 reached Rs. 594.7 billion. Growth in the export segment, which consists of software and IT enabled services such as call centre and back office operations, was especially significant; from Rs. 15.4 billion in 1994 this grew by 30 times to Rs. 461.0 billion in 2002. Export of software and related services greatly contributed to the growth of the software industry. In the late 1990s year on year growth of the export figure reached an average of 62 per cent. A tiny 2 per cent in 1994, the share of exports of total earnings grew to 18 per cent by 2002, and its importance as a source of foreign currency is growing.

The steady growth of the software industry through the 1990s was followed by a sudden slowdown in 2001. The close of the so-called 'year 2000 problem' and 'collapse of the IT bubble' were factors responsible for this. However, the share of related services such as call centre and back office operations for companies in the developed countries began growing after 2000, due to resorting to outsourcing to reduce costs. These trends are allowing us to see the nature of India's software and related services industry which are closely tied to the overseas markets.

The overwhelming majority of India's software and related services exports are to the United States, accounting for 61.1 per cent of the total export value in 2000 (see Table 6.1). Next are the United Kingdom (11.8 per cent), Japan (3.6 per cent), Germany (3.2 per cent), Singapore (1.9 per cent). Compared to other nations, Singapore's economy is small, but despite this it is the fourth largest importer.

Indian software and related services professionals at the end of 1990 numbered 56,000. By the end of 2002 this had ballooned to 6,61,000 people, a 12-fold increase. The numbers include IT Enabled Services, and those not directly involved in software development, such as call centre and back office operations. Even so, the numbers confirm to us that the industry has created job opportunities in a very short period of time and in very large numbers.

As for the labour market, in India while there are relatively few highly skilled software engineers who churn between companies, there is a very high stock of relatively lower skilled human resources that have the potential to become software engineers. Due to the emergence of a large numbers of engineers in a relatively short period, India has very few experienced engineers. For this reason, it is generally held that Indian software engineers do not have the skills to compete in the international market. However, the rapid growth of the software industry

Table 6.1: Major importer of Indian software and services

Country	*Export**	
	(Rs. in crore)	*(Percentage)*
1 USA	17,336	61.1
2 UK	3,355	11.8
3 Japan	1,021	3.6
4 Germany	900	3.2
5 Singapore	540	1.9
6 Canada	425	1.5
7 Belgium	400	1.4
8 Netherlands	360	1.3
9 Switzerland	340	1.2
10 Australia	295	1.0
Others	3,378	11.9
Total	28,350	100.0

Note: * 2000 fiscal year.
Source: NASSCOM, *The IT Industry in India Strategic Review 2002*. New Delhi: NASSCOM, 2002.

provided employment opportunities for even less-experienced, relatively lower-skilled engineers. Also, large software companies have in-house training facilities to improve the technical knowledge of their engineers. That the stock is increasing human resources with a certain degree of technical prowess is important when considering the future growth of India's software industry.

SOFTWARE INDUSTRY POLICY AND REGIONAL BODIES

To deal with the rapid increase in size of the software and related services market, software companies in India have been growing steadily. According to NASSCOM, of its 854 members (in the year 2001), 693 companies whose year of founding could be ascertained. Of these 79 per cent of all member companies were founded after 1991. Coinciding with the IT bubble, 201 software companies were founded in just the two years of 1999 (86 companies) and 2000 (115 companies).

As described above, while being driven by growth of external demand mainly from the United States, the role played by the Indian Government in strengthening the software industry cannot be ignored. Looking at India's software industry policy, the Department of Electronics (DoE) was created in 1970. In 1972, the 'Software Export Scheme' was launched. However, this was done to offer the outflow of foreign currency importing hardware into India. But compared to the late 1980s and 1990s, the activities were extremely passive.

Through restrictions on hardware importation in the years 1980 through 1984, software exports were forced to be temporarily interrupted. The sudden advance in software technology led to the problem of hardware obsolescence. India relied on importing hardware from advanced countries to deal with this problem. Therefore, hardware importation restrictions became an obstacle to infrastructure upgrades for software development and production. As a result, software export sectors lost their ability to compete internationally on technical ability and export revenues fell rapidly.[2]

Soon after coming to power, in 1984, Rajiv Gandhi announced, 'New Computer Policy'. From this point, the software industry was actively nurtured by the central government. With the complementation of the 'Computer Software Export, Software Development and Training Policy' in 1986, software exports again picked up. The benefits of these policies were mainly the deregulation of imports of hardware and software. The hardware tariff was reduced from 135 per cent to 60, and the software tariff was also reduced from 100 per cent to 60. This simplified the importation of hardware into India, and not just made for speedier system upgrades but also lowered the barriers to importing software, mainly operating systems. Through these, not only basic software but also application software production and exports grew rapidly.

Also, smaller size computers made personal computers widespread, and fostered the rise of venture-style small-scale software companies. Furthermore, major Indian corporations turned their software departments into separate companies that would become software exporters. In this way, the switch in export/import policy changed the economic environment surrounding the software industry. And together with lowering the entry barriers for new companies into related industries, the spread of personal computers also spurred establishment of status to give rise to software industry and export industry. Also, in 1991, FDI (foreign direct investment) was actively pursued under the 'New Economic Policy,' and foreign investment flowed into India.

The Software Technology Parks of India (STPI) played an important role in this progress. The STPI was established in 1991 under the DoE, which is under the jurisdiction of the Prime Minister's Office, and is currently falls under jurisdiction of the Ministry of Communication and Information Technology. Its main role is to not so much to build and administer high-tech industrial estates but to establish communications infrastructure such as satellite-based gateways, and administer STPI schemes to provide tax exemption and other benefits for software and related export businesses. The STPI headquarters is in New Delhi, and branch offices are located throughout India to promote the development of satellite communications infrastructure.

One example is the STPI Bangalore located in the 'Electronics City' developed in the Bangalore suburbs by the Karnataka State Electronics Development Corporation Limited (KEONICS). The STPI opened a branch office here in 1991 and set up parabola communication antennas in the industrial estate. This satellite communications facility is the data communications gateway to the world, and services are provided to software and related companies who have arrangements with the STPI. Electronics City has development centres of not just foreign and India companies, but even call centres are located here due to the quality of communications infrastructure. However, STPI's communication services are not limted to Electronics City alone. Through microwave and leased lines, services are provided to companies located in other places within Bangalore.

Also, STPI has branches in other large cities such as NOIDA, Mumbai, Chennai, Hyderabad and Kolkata. In recent years installations are being made in relatively small cities. For instance, as sub-branches of STPI Bangalore, offices are being set up in relatively smaller cities such as Hubli, Mysore, Manipal and Mangalore, where satellite-based gateways are being installed. A communications infrastructure is being put into place for promoting the selling up of software and related companies.

This active stance of the central government to export software and related services has encouraged major foreign corporations, such as AT&T, IBM, Hewlett Packard, Texas Instruments, Intel, Motorola, GE, Siemens, SAP, Sony, Sanyo, Sharp, as well as subsidiaries of Chinese communications companies to locate operations in Bangalore. Also, communications infrastructure established by STPI has eased entry to the software industry for poorly capitalised smaller Indian corporations. In Bangalore it has assisted in the formation of industrial agglomerations not dominated by big foreign firms.

The Karnataka state government, the TATA group, and the Singapore government are together constructing International Technology Park in Bangalore. Many software firms are taking up lease here on the same scale as Electronics City. In response to the government's attitude to export software and positive foreign companies' investment in Indian software industry, both government and private businesses have developed and upgraded physical infrastructure, such as office complexes to attract regional growth opportunities.

SOFTWARE INDUSTRY DISTRIBUTION AND ACCOMPANYING CHANGE

As discussed above, together with regulatory aspects related to export of software, development of communications infrastructure is also being pursued. Even so, India's software industry has a tendency to be located in major cities. Since the 1990s, these software industry agglomerations have grown rapidly (see Figure 6.1).

Of the 693 NASSCOM member companies for which a date of establishment can be discerned, only 51 were founded before full-fledged nurturing of the software industry began in 1984. These were located in major cities—15 were located in Mumbai, 8 in New Delhi, 9 in Bangalore, 3 in Chennai, and 2 each in Kolkata, Pune, Hyderabad and Secunderabad.

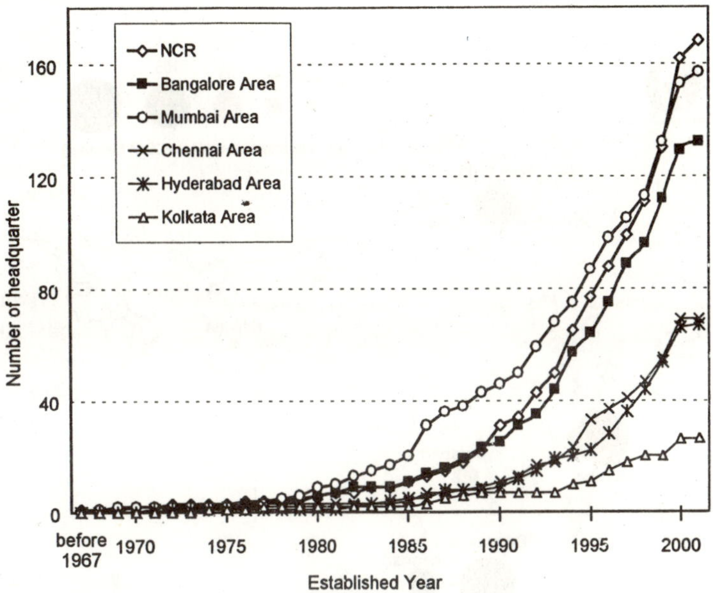

Source: *Indian IT Software and Service Directory*, NASSCOM, 2002.

Figure 6.1: Year of establishment of major software and services firms in India

Until the early 1980s, the software industry was held back by hardware import restrictions, and the number of companies in operation at the time were very few. But as will be discussed later, before the creation of the current six software industrial agglomerations, there were already some software companies located in large cities. Most of these companies were founded with private capital, and demand for software was primarily domestic.

With economic liberalisation, software companies began showing steady yearly growth. In 2001, 132 were located in New Delhi, 152 in Bangalore, 145 in Mumbai, 80 in Chennai, 62 in Hyderabad, and 34 in Kolkata. Also, companies were setting up their headquarters not just in these primary cities but also in states such as Gujarat and Kerala.

Judging from the headquarter locations of NASSCOM member companies, software industry distribution in India is characteristically located in six agglomerations as shown in Figure 6.2. First of these is the National Capital Region (NCR) made up of New Delhi, NOIDA and Gurgaon, and is the largest in India. Second is the Mumbai Area made

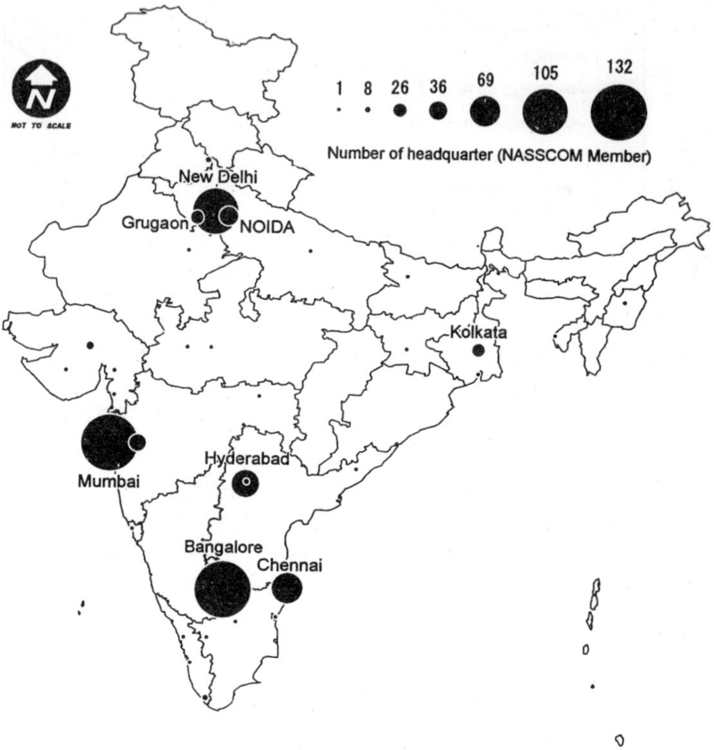

Source: *Indian IT Software and Service Directory*, NASSCOM, 2002.

Figure 6.2: Locational distribution of headquarters of major software and services firms in India

up of Mumbai and Pune, third is the Bangalore Area, fourth is the Chennai Area, fifth is the Hyderabad Area made up of Hyderabad and Secunderabad, and finally the Kolkata Area.

We will now consider in detail the formation process of these six major agglomerations. Figure 6.1 shows the change in the number of companies for each agglomeration. From this, we can see that software companies are increasing in the NCR, Mumbai and Bangalore areas. Through the 1980s, Mumbai Area was India's largest agglomeration. However, when we enter the 1990s, companies preferred the NCR and Bangalore areas, and by the late 1990s NCR grew to the point that it was larger than the Mumbai Area.

After these agglomerations, in terms of growth in the number of companies, the Chennai and Hyderabad agglomerations witnessed inpressive growth. Compared to these, Kolkata Area was relatively flat, but in the late 1990s company establishment has grown largely. Especially for Andhra Pradesh which contains the Hyderabad Area, the state government's encouragements led to growth ot the software industry in the state. In 1998 the Microsoft Corporation's Software Development Centre opened in Hyderabad. The efforts of Andhra Pradesh also affected other states, and based on this learning experience, from the late 1990s other states also actively pursued software and related industry promotion policies at the state government level.

As seen above, until the 1980s, the Mumbai Area stood out as the main software industry agglomeration. However, as we enter the 1990s which was a period of rapid growth for the industry, NCR and the Bangalore Area also witnessed rapid expansion and in the late 1990s agglomerations began to form in Hyderabad, Chennai and Kolkata areas. However the rate of growth varied between each agglomeration. We look at the factors behind these regional differences analysing export trends, which is characteristic of India's software industry.

EXPORT EARNINGS OF SOFTWARE COMPANIES

As can be seen from Table 6.2 showing the export earnings of the software industry in the six primary regions, companies located in south India have higher export rates. Especially for the rising Hyderabad Area, which has an export ratio of 96 per cent, and Secunderabad which has an even higher ratio of 98 per cent. This can be attributed to the effect of a large-scale Indian software company locating its headquarters in Secunderabad. The next region in terms of export ratio is the Bangalore Area (export ratio of 92 per cent). An impressive 38 per cent of all software firms here are export oriented. The export ratio for the Chennai Area is 90 per cent, and 37 per cent of companies are complete software export companies.

The export ratios for the Mumbai and Kolkata areas are lower than the national average; 26 per cent of companies in the Mumbai Area are 100 per cent software export companies and for Kolkata this figure is 31 per cent. For the Mumbai Area, even though the total sales value per company is large, the export ratio is low, and compared to agglomerations in south India, we can see that software companies located here are basing their business on the domestic market.

NCR's export ratio is slightly above the national average, but when we look more closely, we see differences between NOIDA and New

Table 6.2: Export situation of software and services industry in major cities

Industrial agglomeration	*Revenue per firm** (*Rs. in Million*)	*Export per firm** (*Rs. in Million*)	*Share of Export** (*Percentage*)
NCR	813	723	89
New Delhi	301	196	65
NOIDA	2,192	2,107	96
Gurgaon	217	179	83
Mumbai Area	854	707	83
Mumbai	1,065	879	83
Pune	242	209	86
Bangalore Area	526	486	92
Chennai Area	753	679	90
Hyderabad Area	355	341	96
Hyderabad	104	95	92
Secunderabad	2,564	2,501	98
Kolkata Area	112	99	88
India	628	552	88

Note: * 2000 fiscal year.
Source: *The IT Industry in India: Strategic Review 2002*, New Delhi: NASSCOM, 2002.

Delhi. The export ratio for New Delhi is relatively low, at 65 per cent. This could be because many software companies appear to have located themselves in New Delhi to fill private company and government demand in the capital of New Delhi. In contrast, the export ratio for NOIDA is 96 per cent, which is same as that of Hyderabad. Since NOIDA was developed as an industrial estate, it was easier to obtain land here than in New Delhi. For this reason, it appears that some companies are exporting software and related services while performing labour-intensive development and production. Overall, then, export-oriented companies have a tendency to be concentrated in south India, while software companies satisfying domestic demand tend to be formed in software agglomerations such as Mumbai and New Delhi.

India's software industry experienced enormous growth in the 1990s to meet overseas demand, but after the collapse of the so-called 'IT bubble', the industry is seeking a new growth model. In this context, the next move by India's software industry should be interesting to watch.

NOTES

1 NASSCOM, *The IT Industry in India Strategic Review 2002*, New Delhi: NASSCOM, 2002, p. 136.

2 R. Heeks, *India's Software Industry: State Policy, Liberalisation and Industrial Development*, New Delhi: Sage, 1996, p. 428.

PART III

INDUSTRIAL ESTATE DEVELOPMENT AND INDUSTRIALISATION IN BACKWARD AREAS

CHAPTER 7

Development of Pithampur Industrial Growth Centre

HIDENORI OKAHASHI

OVERVIEW OF MADHYA PRADESH

Madhya Pradesh (MP)[1] is among largest states of India, but, its population of 66.18 million people (1991 census) is relatively small. Compared to India's overall population density of 267 people/sq km, MP's population density of 149 people/sq km is relatively low. However, the state's population is growing at a rapid rate, and 1981 and 1991 exceeded India's national growth rate. Its natural growth rate of 24.4 per cent (1990) is the highest nationally, and a high birth rate is likely behind this population growth.

Most of the state is situated atop the high plateau leading to the Deccan Plateau. Partly due to the low irrigated arable land ratio and susceptibility to drought, agricultural productivity is low. However, 46 per cent of the state's GDP depends on agricultural production, and because industrial sector contribution to state revenues is still below the national average, per capita income is low, highlighting the backward state of the economy.

From an all-India perspective, MP is notable as a poor region in the 'Hindi Belt'. It is also in the 'Tribal Belt', which cuts India's central region into east and west. To overcome this low rate of development, MP implemented several industrial development policies. One of these was the setting up of industrial estates called industrial growth centres, which aimed to promote growth through industrialisation by courting companies to locate there. Pithampur Industrial Growth Centre, the subject of our study, is the largest of these industrial estates and can be regarded as an industrial development success story.

EVOLUTION OF INDUSTRIAL DEVELOPMENT POLICY AND LOCATIONAL CONDITIONS OF INDUSTRY

Growth of Industrial Development Policy

During the colonial era, MP had only a small consumable goods industry producing items such as furniture, textiles, processed sugar and leather products. Although there were rich mineral deposits in the east and south, there was hardly any heavy industry that took advantage of these resources. Only the Malwa region in the western part of the state produced cotton that attracted interest, and the latter half of the nineteenth century saw the concentration of cotton spinning industry around Indore.

By the time of independence industrialisation had occurred on a limited scale, and after independence, the furthering of industrial development in MP was entirely dependent on public corporations. Typical of these was the Bhilai steel works, one of the largest steel plants in India, which located in the eastern part of the state, and the BHEL factory in Bhopal.

While industrial agglomeration continued around the main cities in the western part of the state, companies in the eastern part were disproportionately of the type which needed to be located close to raw materials, resulting in regional disparity. The Sixth Five-Year Plan (1980-5) aimed to correct this imbalance by encouraging investment which would set up industries in backward areas development of industrial growth centres. Also, to improve convenience for companies moving to backward districts, MPAKVN (MP State Industrial Centre Development Corporation) furthered progress toward a single point of contact for industrial development. By the Seventh Five Year Plan (1985-90), results began to be seen; 15 of 18 'No Industry Districts' succeeding in attracting at least one large or medium scale factory. This was also the period when India's economy was partially liberalised.

After the full-fledged economic liberalisation policies of 1991, MP announced its 'Industry Policy and Action Plan' (1994) which aimed to attract investment, develop regions equally, create employment opportunities, and improve living standards. These objectives showed an even greater level of willingness on the state's part to take steps to promote industrialisation. Today, MPs high rate of growth is attracting attention at the national level.

Locational Conditions for Industry

Listed below are five advantages of locating one's industry in MP. (1) Its central location in India is advantageous for acquiring resources and delivering products to market. The western part of the state borders the development axis connecting Delhi and Mumbai, tempting companies to move into MP from developed regions such as Maharashtra, Gujarat and Delhi. (2) There is access to plentiful and quality workforce. (3) The state is actively pursuing policies to attract industry. In addition to concessions such as reduced taxes and subsidies, systematic responses are being made to attract companies. (4) There are rich mineral deposits around the eastern part of the state. (5) As evident in soybean farming and processing, there are developed commercial farming and agricultural processing industries.

Of these, (3) is of special interest. An organisation independent from the state government has been established whose function is to develop industrial growth centres, attract industry, and integrate administration and management functions. This organisation was called MPAVN (MP State Industrial Development Corporation). The organisation directly responsible for industrial growth centre development, there are separate MPAKVNs for each of the six region. MPAVN is owned by the state government and the MPAKVN are its subsidiaries, both are public corporations. MPAKVN does not only concern itself with commercial infrastructure but also works to improve social infrastructure and various services required by companies and workers. Furthermore, in cooperation with the state government is responsible for activities such as marketing and sales of industrial plots, maintenance, administration and management of various facilities.

The problems industries faec in setting up plants in MP are: (1) outdated infrastructure (especially electricity and water), (2) shortage of skilled labour, (3) industrial policy being decided by an elite minority. Poor infrastructure is a problem anywhere in India, but (2) and (3) are especially prominent problems in a backward region like MP.

Finally, potential problems that may be encountered when attempting to set up industry are: (1) labour movement, (2) political instability due to strained political party relations, and (3) risk of state budget collapse due to the high burden of subsidy. Excluding (3), (1) and (2) are common problems throughout India, and are likely to remain concerns for future economic growth.

INDUSTRIAL GROWTH CENTRES: DEVELOPMENT

Development Area Zoning

To encourage industrial growth throughout the state, the MP government operates a graded scale incentive system that favours companies which locate in backward areas. All 45 districts are categorised as developed or backward districts based on their level of development, and bigger tax breaks and longer periods of tax exemption are granted to companies moving into the more backward districts (see Table 7.1). Additionally, companies can earn additional benefits if they move into state-developed industrial estates.

Table 7.1: MP state investment subsidy (revised in 1989)

Category	*Rate (% of fixed investment)*	*Maximun ceiling in Rs. lakhs*	
		Small scale industry	*Middle/Large scale industry*
Advanced district	5.0	–	–
Backward district 'A'	7.5	1.5	5.0
Backward district 'B'	10.0	2.0	7.0
Backward district 'C'	10.0	2.5	10.0
Growth centre	15.0	5.0	15.0

Source: MPAKVN (Indore).

Regions are categorised according to the level of development, as shown in Figure 7.1. There are only five developed districts (Bhopal, Indore, Gwalior, Jabalpur, and Durg), and these districts are made up of either primary cities or districts which already have industrial areas. Bhopal, the state capital (population 1.06 million in 1991), and Indore, the textile city (1.1 million people) are the state's political, commercial, and industrial hubs. Other important cities include Gwalior in the northern part of the state (7,20,000 people) and Jabalpur in the central part of the state (8,87,000 people). These four cities function as regional hubs, as their influence expands beyond the districts in which they are located.

Districts other than the five mentioned above are all backward, and are further subdivided according to their level of development into Category A (12 districts), Category B (5 districts) and Category C (23 districts). From Figure 7.1 we see that relatively more developed districts lie between Indore and Bhopal, and between Jabalpur and Durg. However, looking more closely, we find that even these core developed districts are frequently bordered by Category C backward districts, revealing the

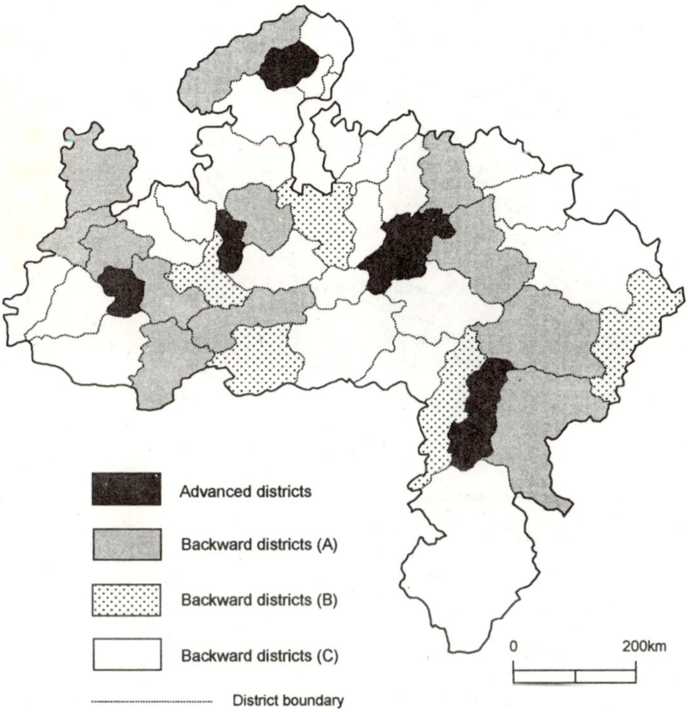

Source: MPAKVN (Indore).

Figure 7.1: District-wise development category in MP

extreme disparity between regions even on the smallest scale.

Let us consider this developmental disparity together with the transportation network shown in Figure 7.2. The most important development corridor for MP is the National Highway 3, which passes through the western part of the state. National Highway 3 is the backbone of the region connecting Mumbai, Agra and Delhi, and is a principal road with high flow of goods. Cities such as Gwalior and Indore which sit on this road benefit from it. The major cities and industrial areas of MP how excellent transportation infrastructure, but the western part of the state is most conveniently located.

Industrial Growth Centre Locations and Regional Differences

As of 1995, there were a total of 21 industrial growth centres in MP (see Figure 7.3). Their locations were closely related to MP's regional

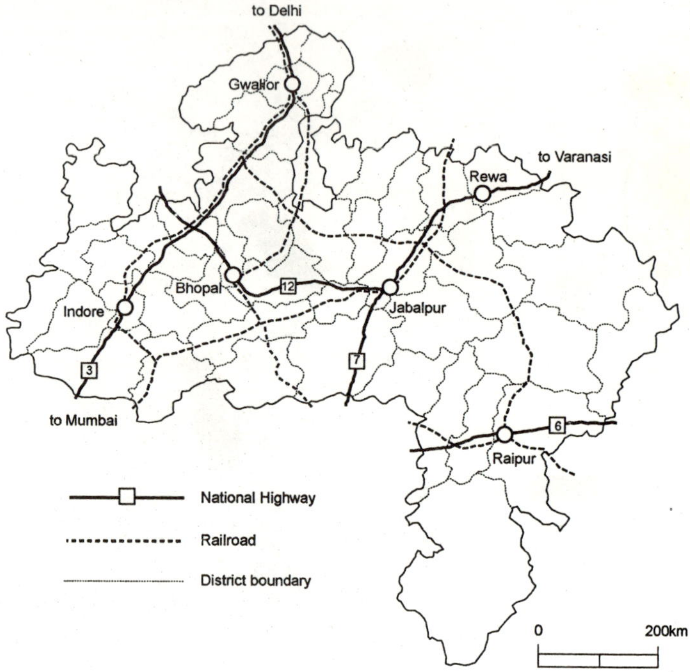

Figure 7.2: Main traffic lines in MP

structure, discussed above. As previously discussed, India's industrial development policies encouraged industry to move from large cities to backward regions, based on the strategy that these industries would serve as magnets for growth in these backward regions. However, because India's backward regions have little existing industrial base and poor infrastructure, problems in site location faced by incoming industries are great. In reality, therefore, most of these industries are located in sites that neighbour and depend on existing urban concentrations.

This tendency is evident in MP as well. All 21 industrial growth centres are located in backward districts, but most of these have been developed in districts that neighbour developed districts. The largest of these are located along the border with advanced districts. Growth centres away from developed districts, tend to be small with sale of plots not progressing as well as it could. This is especially evident in industrial growth centres in the eastern part of the state. Since there are few companies moving to this region, benefits of industrial growth centres are limited here.

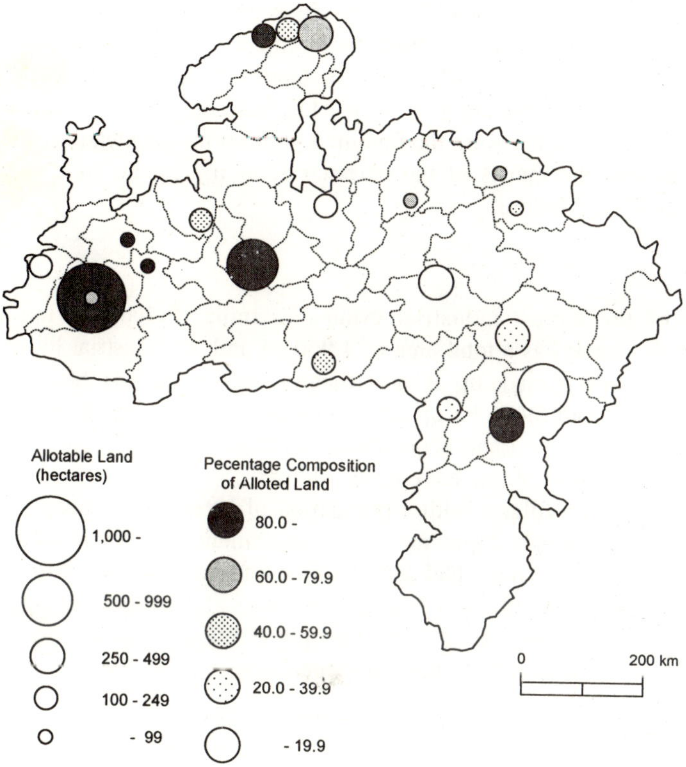

Source: MPAKVN (Indore).

Figure 7.3: Distribution of industrial growth centres in MP

PITHAMPUR INDUSTRIAL GROWTH CENTRE: DEVELOPMENT

Location

Dhar district, where Pithampur Industrial Growth Centre is established, had a high population of Scheduled Tribes and Other Backward Castes; its economic activity was centred around agriculture and the growth rate was low. Its backwardness is reflected in its 'Backward Area: Category C5' and 'No Industry District' rankings, and until the 1970s it was a region untouched by industrial development.

The setting up of industrial growth centres required two conditions to be area: the location must be a backward district; secondly, the location must be at least 15 km away from cities of 7,50,000 to 1.5 million people (1981 census). Both requirements were met because Dhar district is a backward district and Pithampur village is 35 km away from Indore. Actually, Pithampur is only 2 km from the district boundary for Indore. So while enjoying the favoured policies for backward districts, it also enjoys the merits of the external economy of the state's largest industrial city, Indore.

Overview

One of the largest industrial estates in India, Pithampur Industrial Growth Centre has a total area of 1,960 ha and an industrial lot area of 1,372 ha, and is made up of three sectors (see Figure 7.4). Sector 1 was developed from 594.6 ha of farmland and wasteland which surrounded Pithampur village. Land acquisition was done from 1983 to 1984, and 416 ha of industrial lots have been sold out.

Pithampur village, with a population of barely 1,286 people (1981 census) before development, was a settlement that revolved around agriculture and at most had a post office and health clinic. After development, with the influx of industrial workers and general labourers, the population quickly rose to 11,980 people (1991 census) and the village is slowly integrating with the industrial estate.

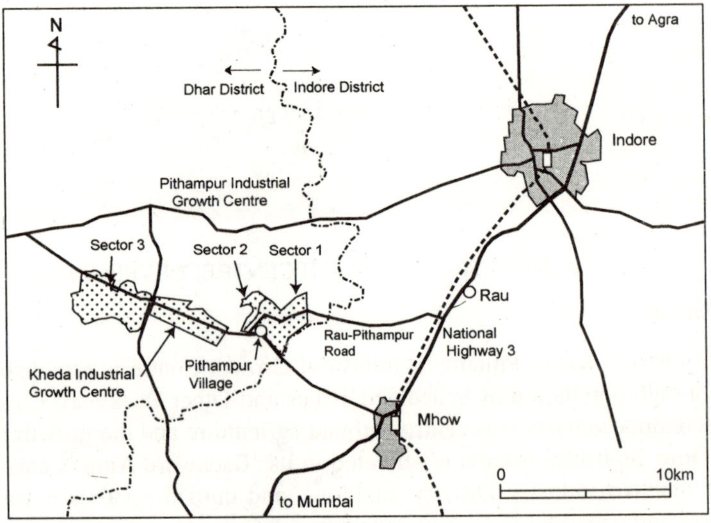

Figure 7.4: Location of Pithampur Industrial Growth Centre

Sector 2 was 117 ha of government owned hilly land behind Sector 1 that was repurposed for industrial use: Sectors 1 and 2 function as a unit in terms of sharing infrastructures. As will be shown in the next chapter, these two sectors have lots of various sizes and these are targeted for factories of varied scales. The industrial lots for Sector 1 are mostly sold out, but scattered vacant lots can be seen. On some lots construction of factory buildings has not even begun.

Sector 3 is approximately 7 km away from Sector 2, and its total area is 1,170 ha. Because this sector was developed relatively recently, most factories located here after the 1990s. Industrial water and power supply is provided separately from the supplies for Sectors 1 and 2.

A wide agricultural belt comes between Sectors 1, 2 and 3. In 1989 when a new development project called Kheda Industrial Growth Centre was approved by the Central Government, which is changing the Pithampur picture. This project officially is a separate project, but in reality it functions as if it were an extension of Pithampur Industrial Growth Centre, emphasising the connections between the centre's existing infrastructure and companies located here. Kheda Industrial Growth Centre as of 1995 has only been developed up to 140 ha, but it is a project with a planned area of 1,039 ha. Together with Pithampur Industrial Growth Centre, this area will eventually emerge as one of India's biggest industrial spaces.

As of 1995, there were 98 large and medium scale industrial factories and 237 small scale factories in operation in Pithampur Industrial Growth Centre, making it the largest industrial area in MP. Industries located here are mainly those targeting the national market for machinery, automobiles, chemicals and plastics as well as steel and electric/electronic devices. Notably, four automobile makers have moved here, forming an automobile industrial area that includes component manufacturers. Because this industrial area was formed during the partial economic liberalisation phase of the 1980s, one notable characteristic is the low number of factories established through foreign capital and foreign technical tie-ups.

SIGNIFICANCE OF AND PROBLEMS IN INDUSTRIAL GROWTH CENTRE DEVELOPMENT

From the 1980s through the 1990s, MP experienced rapid industrial growth. This attracted much attention in India that it was ever covered in leading magazines. Actually, the industrial agglomeration at Pithampur

Industrial Growth Centre was successful for the most part in attracting factories. From a Japanese perspective, it seems odd that Eicher Mitsubishi and Kinetic Honda would choose to locate large factories in Pithampur, riddled infrastructure problems. Clearly, preferential treatment for companies through development area zoning had a large role in decisions to locate factories at places like these. Furthermore, because approval from the Central Government was required to open factories, there must have been some kind of encouragement to set up base in Pithampur. On the other hand, the state government took great effort to make companies' site location convenient by setting up a single organisation for activities related to factory development. However, it is probably not possible to repeat the success of Pithampur at other places within the state. If we look at the occupancy rates for industrial growth centres, there are clear regional differences, and while estates bordering the national axis (national highway corridor) through the western part of the state have been popular, eastern regions remain stagnant with low occupancies. Therefore, the problem is regional differences within the state.

Pithampur benefited from the preferential policies for backward districts and also enjoyed the effects of the external economy of the neighbouring industrial city Indore, the largest in the state. Also, this development centre, which was the largest scale even in India, can be regarded as part of a regional growth strategy to take Indore, which was historically the textile centre but mired in low growth, to a new economic level.

Follwing full-fledged economic liberalisation in 1991, an increasing number of factories funded with foreign capital are being located in metropolitan areas such as Delhi, Mumbai and Chennai. Will these changing conditions threaten MP's industrial development strategy? This will be an interesting area to watch out for the future.

NOTE

1 In 2000 the eastern portion of Madhya Pradesh was made into the new state of Chhattisgarh. However we are based on the previous territory of the state. It is mainly because our survey was conducted before 2000.

CHAPTER 8

Infrastructure for New Industrial Estates

TAKESHI MINAMINO

THE 'INFRASTRUCTURE BOTTLENECK'

'Infrastructure bottleneck' is a widely known problem of India.[1] This has greatly impacted the country's industrial growth. Electricity supply is the most obvious example. Electricity supply lags an average of 10 per cent behind demand during normal consumption periods, and almost 20 per cent behind demand during peak times. In addition to electricity, other infrastructure such as roads, rail, ports, telecommunications, water supply and sewage, housing, schools and hospitals are also short supply. Therefore, to equip industrial estates with sufficient infrastructure becomes an important issue in industrial development. Development of industrial estates especially in backward districts where infrastructure is least developed, becomes an ever more significant issue.

In this chapter, we will look into how infrastructure in new industrial estates is established and managed, and how incoming factories respond to the provided supply of water and electricity. Pithampur Industrial Growth Centre, which is located in a backward district is examined here as a case study.

THE DEVELOPER: MPAKVN (INDORE)

The lack of basic infrastructure has been pointed out as an obstacle to industrial development in backward districts in India. At Pithampur Industrial Growth Centre, MPAKVN (Indore) has worked to provide infrastructure and attract corporates.

The planned investment estimated for Pithampur Industrial Growth Centre was Rs. 110 million. Of this, Rs. 40 million was to come from the state government, Rs. 50 million was to have been borrowed from the Industrial Development Bank of India (IDBI), and the remaining

Table 8.1: Expenditure on development of Pithampur Industrial Growth Centre (1990)

Item	*(Rs. in million)*	%
Land acquistion	117.9	31.8
Water supply	84.9	22.9
Power station	54.0	14.5
Roads & culverts	42.3	11.4
Sheds	28.3	7.6
Housing	15.2	4.1
Street light	8.5	2.3
Fire station	8.0	2.2
Amenities	5.0	1.3
Police station	3.0	0.8
School building	1.7	0.5
Plantation	1.5	0.4
Hospital	1.0	0.3
Total	371.1	100.0

Source: MPAKVN (Indore).

Rs. 20 million was to have been provided aid by the central government. The money was to have been recovered from profits generated through activities such as land sales.

However, according to the statement of expenses as of June 1990, the actual total expenses by MPAKVN (Indore) for Pithampur Industrial Growth Centre was Rs. 371.1 million, more than three times the originally planned amount. The breakdown of these expenses is shown in Table 8.1. The greatest expense has been land acquisition cost, which accounts for 31.8 per cent of the total. Expenses for water supply are 22.9 per cent, for electricity supply 14.5 per cent, and for roads & culverts 11.4 per cent. These costs for industrial infrastructure make up the greater part of the total expense. There are also expenses for infrastructure for living, such as housing, cultural facilities, schools and hospitals. The development of Pithampur is unique in that it includes industrial infrastructure as well as living infrastructure. In other words, MPAKVN's plan helps promote the overall development of the backward district.

WATER SUPPLY BY MPAKVN (INDORE)

The planned water demand for Pithampur Industrial Growth Centre is 337.5 million litres per day for industrial use and 135 million litres per day for domestic use. The water supply for Pithampur Industrial Growth Centre is managed by MPAKVN (Indore). The source of this water supply is reservoirs and tube wells. There are two reservoirs built by constructing dams across rivers. Both were constructed by the Irrigation Department of MP state. These dams are multipurpose; they provide water to not only Pithampur Industrial Growth Centre but also the surrounding areas for irrigation. 22 tube wells have been dug inside the industrial centre by MPAKVN (Indore) itself until now. Only 4 have sufficient water reserves.

To acquire water connections within Pithampur Industrial Growth Centre, companies must enter into a contract with MPAKVN (Indore). At the registration, they are required to pay an entry fee, a contract fee and a deposit which varies depending upon the volume of contracted water. The requestor is also billed for actual water use.

Water bills are divided into two types; industrial use and domestic use. The water rate for industrial use is divided into two categories, filtered and unfiltered water. The former is Rs. 9 per 1,000 litres; the latter is Rs. 7.5. For filtered water, the rate was originally set at Rs. 2.5 per 1,000 litres, but was latter increased and eventually became Rs. 9 in 1996. The national average rate for industrial water in Japan is ¥ 17.0 per 1,000 litres. Since the rupee/yen conversion rate at the time this information was gathered was Re. 1 = ¥ 3.2, Rs. 9 per 1,000 litres is equal to ¥ 28.8 per 1,000 litres. Thus the water rate in India is very high compared to Japan.

Water for domestic use, on the other hand, is billed at a fixed monthly rate of Rs. 30 for customers without meters or Rs. 2 per 1,000 litres for customers with meters.

PREPARING FACTORIES FOR SECURING WATER AND ELECTRICITY

We surveyed 21 factories on securing water and electricity in Pithampur Industrial Growth Centre. The result showed that 17 of 21 factories had their own water supply facilities, and 11 of 21 had their own electricity generation facilities. This indicates that factories cannot be run only with the infrastructure provided by MPAKVN (Indore). Consequently, by taking Factory A, which has its own water and electricity facilities, as a case study, we would like to look at how factories in Pithampur meet water and electricity requirements.

Factory A manufactures scooters. It was founded in 1986. With

1,071 employees (as of November 1997), it was one of the largest factories in Pithampur Industrial Growth Centre.

Water

To manufacture a scooter needs 1,003 litres of water. Factory A requires approximately 4,00,000 litres of water daily. However, its contract with MPAKVN (Indore) is only for 2,50,000 litres per day. Thus the factory supplies the remaining 1,50,000 litres from its own water sources on an ongoing basis.

Figure 8.1 shows the amount of water Factory A received from MPAVKN (Indore) every month in the three years from November 1993 to October 1996. It also shows the monthly average share of water sources during these three years. There is no specific trend apparent in terms of the annual amount of water supplied from MPAKVN (Indore). When looking at the amount of water received monthly, it is low from October to January every year. Here, we can observe seasonal trends.

Now, we would like to consider the significance of this seasonality. Pithampur and its basin are heavily affected by the Southwest monsoons. The annual rainfall averages 1,000 mm, and 90 per cent of this falls during the monsoon season between June and September. Thus, it can be said that the water supply is relatively stable during these months. During the post-monsoon season from October to December, rainfall decreases. However because the monsoon rainfall has accumulated in

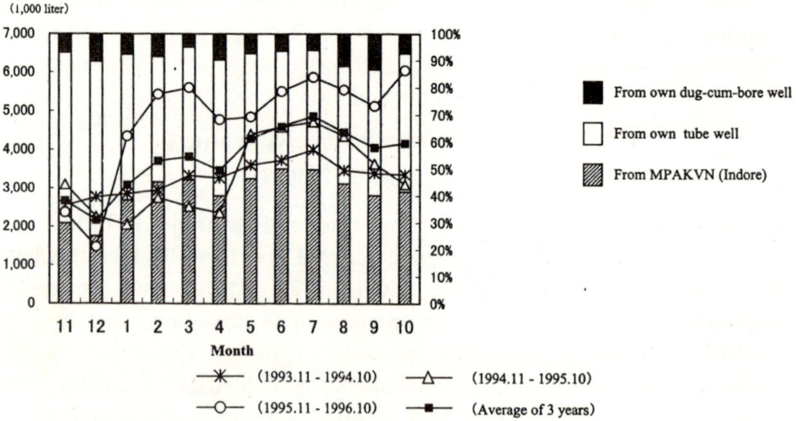

Source: Field survey in 1996.

Figure 8.1: Water supply from MPAKVN (Indore) and percentage of water sources in Factory A

dams, this period also can be thought of as having a relatively stable water supply. That is to say the water supply is most scarce in the pre-monsoon season which is from March to May. The water supply received from March to May is less than during the monsoon months, but it is more than the amount of water supplied during the post-monsoon season. Even though the post-monsoon season should have a relatively stable water supply due to the water stored in the dams, the amount of water received from October to December and the following January is in fact extremely low.

This is because October to January is the irrigation season for *Rabi* crops in this region. The conflict between industry and agriculture is one factor behind the decrease in water supply between October and January. This friction with agriculture is not just limited to water but extends to struggles over electricity as discussed later.

What do factories do to deal with the shortage water? Factory A dug its first tube well in 1985 (96 m deep, 12,000 litres/hour) and second in 1988 (105 m deep, 6,000 litres/hour). It opened a dug-cum-bore well in 1992 (15 m deep, 7,000 litres/hour), and in 1995 opened two tub ewells simultaneously (each 84 m deep, 10,000 litres/hour). It now has four tube wells and one dug-cum-bore well as its own water sources.

In terms of proportion of water sources, 41.5 per cent of water is provided by MPAKVN (Indore), 8.5 per cent from its own dug-cum-bore well, and 50 per cent from its tube wells (see Figure 8.1). During the months when supply is more received from MPAKVN (Indore), the proportion of own water sources decreases, and when the amount supplied by MPAKVN (Indore) is low, the proportion of own water sources is high. In December, when the supply from MPAKVN (Indore) is at the lowest, the proportion of water used from own water sources reaches 75 per cent.

The above findings indicate that the water supply from MPAKVN (Indore) is insufficient and unstable. Also, the factories are relying on their own private sources to make up for the insufficient and unstable water supply. Furthermore, when the water supply becomes insufficient due to the overall water shortage—not due to the conflict with agriculture—like a decrease of stored water in the reservoirs in the pre-monsoon season, factories often become incapable of meeting their water needs through their own sources. Factory A, for example, purchases water from farmers. This purchased water comes from wells of nearby farms (mostly tube wells drilled for irrigation purposes). The going rate at the time of the field survey was Rs. 22 per 1,000 litres.

Electricity

Electricity is indispensable in manufacturing. Factory A requires 50.9 kWh of electricity for each scooter it produces. Here again, we would like to focus on Factory A's achievements in securing electrical power for the period from November 1993 to October 1996.

As shown in Figure 8.2, Factory A's electricity supply comes from both MPEB and self-generation. For self-generation, Factory A owns three generators with a total production capacity of 2.5 MWh. Some 70.2 per cent of its electrical power comes from MPEB and 29.8 per cent from its own generators. Compared to water supply, the ratio of self-supply in electricity is lower.

The trend of electricity supplied by MPEB shows the same kind of pattern seen in the water supplied by MPAKVN (Indore). The electricity supply decreases between October and January, and also in June. The dip in June is caused by a fall in hydroelectric power generation, the main source of electrical power for this region, as the water in dams is at their lowest levels during the pre-monsoon season. During the lean months, the ratio of self-generated power increases. In November, which has the lowest supply from MPEB, the ratio of self-generated power is 50.5 per cent.

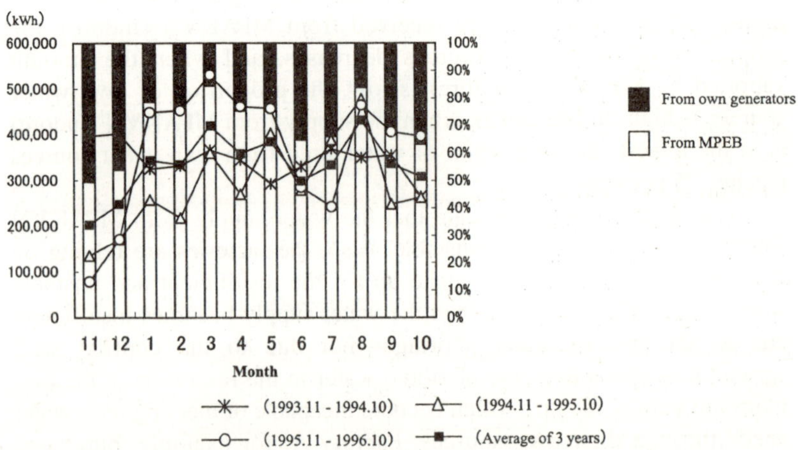

Source: Field survey in 1996.

Figure 8.2: Electricity supply from MPEB and percentage of sources of power in Factory A

The friction between industry and agriculture is also a factor in this trend. This is because irrigation in this region is largely dependent on tubewells and electric pumps are used for pumping water from the wells. Therefore during the peak irrigation period from October to January, electricity demand for agriculture becomes the highest.

Furthermore, the fall in electric power supply is closely related to the decrease in water supply from MPAKVN (Indore). Pithampur Industrial Growth Centre's water supply system first stores water in overhead tanks, after receiving it from its water sources, and then uses natural flow to distribute it. Electricity is used to pump up water into these overhead tanks. Also, to transfer water from one reservoir, electric pumps are used to cross the watershed boundary. This consumes large amounts of electricity. In this way, the shortfall in electricity supply makes the water problem more severe.

CHARACTERISTICS AND NEW TRENDS OF INFRASTRUCTURE DEVELOPMENT IN INDIA

Based on what we have learned from Pithampur Industrial Growth Centre, we would like to cite two characteristics and a new trend in the provision of infrastructure for industrial estate development in India.

1. *Regional Overall Development by MPAKVN (Indore)*

The construction of Pithampur Industrial Growth Centre carries great significance for regional development in backward districts. The operations of MPAKVN (Indore), which was responsible for Pithampur's development, are concerned not only with industrial infrastructure directly related to manufacturing, but also extend to providing infrastructure for the living environment, such as cultural facilities and hospitals. This sort of regional development done by the industrial developer is a distinctive feature of industrial estate development in India.

2. *Insufficient Infrastructure and Private Solutions*

Electricity shortage in India is severe, with the demand exceeding supply by 10 per cent during normal periods and the shortfall approaching 20 per cent during peak periods. For this reason, factories in India generally maintain their own electric power generation facilities. An average 17 per cent of electricity consumed by factories is self-generated.[2] For Factory A, the self-generation ratio is 29.8 per cent, higher than the national average. Likewise, the ratio of own water supply is also high.

The poor state of infrastructure and functional shortcomings are unavoidable realities at Pithampur Industrial Growth Centre. However, each factory has taken individual steps to deal with these shortcomings, and non-public alternatives are also pursued, such as purchasing water from farmers . The current private solutions do lead to great social losses and shortage of capital which makes public works maintenance difficult. But the coexistence of publicly provided infrastructure and supplemental private solutions is one notable characteristic of industrial estate development in India today.

3. *A New Trend*

Finally, we would like to highlight a new trend in infrastructure development seen at Pithampur Industrial Growth Centre. This is the construction of toll roads by private companies. Previously, travel to Pithampur from Indore required a circuitous route via National Highway 3 from Indore to Mhow, and then on to Pithampur via State Highway 27. However, by opening a link directly connecting Indore to Pithampur via Rau, which lies between Indore and Mhow, the distance to Indore has been shortened by 10 km.

The private company Infrastructure Leasing & Financial Services Limited (IL&FS) played a central role in this construction. In order to utilise private capital and technology, the MP state government in May 1994 allowed private capital in infrastructure development projects.[3] Soon after, IL&FS joined the Rau-Pithampur Road Construction Project, investing Rs. 40 million and completing the 11.5 km bypass. IL&FS hopes to recover its investment capital within 12 years by collecting toll tax.

This trend to involve private companies in infrastructure development is now seen nationwide in India. To supplement shortfalls in road construction funds, India's central government and state governments are planning road construction with external and internal capital according to the BOT (Build, Operate, Transfer) method. As of April 1994, 27 projects construction of toll bypasses, bridges and expressways have been opened to private companies in cluding foreign ones.[4] Expectations of foreign and private investment in electrical power and telecommunications are also high.[5] The participation of private capital is a positive trend when considering the future of India's infrastructure.

NOTES

1 H. Ishigami, 'Infrastructure', in S. Ito (ed.), *Indo no Kougyouka* (*Industrialisation in India*), Tokyo: Institute of Developing Economies, 1988, pp. 140-51.
2 S. Ito and H. Esho, *Tachiagaru Indo Keizai* (*Economic Development of India*), Tokyo: Nihon Keizai Shimbun, 1995, p. 199.
3 Government of Madhya Pradesh, *Industrial Policy and Action Plan 1994.*
4 Ito and Esho, *Tachiagaru Indo Keizai*, pp. 195-6.
5 Ibid., pp. 200-3.

CHAPTER 9

Structure of Industrial Agglomeration in Pithampur: Automobile and Related Industries

KAZUO TOMOZAWA

PROCESS OF INDUSTRIAL AGGLOMERATION AND CHARACTERISTICS OF FACTORIES

As of 1995, 98 large and medium scale industries and 237 small-scale industries were located at Pithampur Industrial Growth Centre. The categorisation of large and medium and small scale is based on the capital invested for each factory.

Companies began to move to Pithampur around 1986 when Sectors 1 and 2 were completed. Until 1986, four automakers were located here who became symbols of industrialisation at this site. Subsequently related subcontracting factories began to flow in one after the other.

When looking at the small-scale industry, 1987 was the peak of establishment, and after this time the number of firms opening factories has been falling. The reduction has been consistent since the 1990s, and now the influx of factories can be said to have levelled off. During the economic crisis of the early 1990s, corporations planning new factories hesitated to put their plans into action. This was a factor that widely limited the appearance of factories of the type that would spawn subcontractor related industries like those seen in the early years. However, with the recovery of the Indian economy from about 1993, companies showed increased interest in investment, and the production output of existing companies at the site also steadily grew. As a result, there were 16 new large and medium scale industries in 1995, a new record, sparking hopes for an investment recovery.

Table 9.1 shows number of businesses and number of employees as of 1995, broken down based on the factory / industry classification. Pithampur's characteristics became apparent when compared to industries all over MP. There are notable factories in MP such as the

Table 9.1: Outline of industrial units in Pithampur, 1995

Industries	*No. of units*				*No. of employment*			
	M/L	*SSI*	*Total*	*(%)*	*M/L*	*SSI*	*Total*	*(%)*
Engineering/Automobile	16	56	72	(21.5)	3,633	1,521	5,154	(20.7)
Textile	10	9	19	(5.7)	3,680	256	3,936	(15.8)
Pharmaceuticals	8	12	20	(6.0)	1,628	849	2,477	(10.0)
Food/Agriculture	5	6	11	(3.3)	356	129	485	(1.9)
Iron/Steel	13	34	47	(14.0)	1,822	1,546	3,368	(13.5)
Cement	3	2	5	(1.5)	155	122	277	(1.1)
Chemical/Plastic	23	51	74	(22.1)	2,323	1,216	3,539	(14.2)
Packaging	2	13	15	(4.5)	326	333	659	(2.6)
Electrical/Electronic	12	29	41	(12.2)	2,208	1,131	3,339	(13.4)
Others	6	25	31	(9.3)	842	803	1,645	(6.6)
Total	98	237	335	(100.0)	16,973	7,906	24,879	(100.0)

Note: M/L: medium and large scale industries, SSI: small scale industry.
Source: MPAKVN (Indore).

Bhilai steel works, but the majority are small-scale factories targeting mainly local markets or existing foodstuffs and furniture markets. There were 8,894 factories in MP in 1989; of these 31.9 per cent made furniture and 31.3 per cent were in the food industry. On the other hand, the percentage for machinery sector was less than 3 per cent for each of general machinery, electric equipment, and transportation equipment, as well as for factories in the heavy and chemical industries. Therefore, in terms of number of factories, MP still was dominated by traditional industries, and modern industries had not made much inroads.

On the other hand, factories at Pithampur were dominated by chemicals/plastics (22.1 per cent), machinery/automobiles (21.5 per cent), steel (14.0 per cent), and electrics/electronics (12.2 per cent). Compared to the furniture and foodstuffs mentioned earlier, Pithampur's tenants have a wider background with many finished products targeting the national market. Also, as seen in the automobile and electric/electronic segments, many of these factories have operations spread across different companies and industries. Evident in its new name 'India's Detroit', the formation of an industrial region which brought together automobile makers and their related factories was planned into Pithampur from the beginning. The contrast of existing industries with local characteristics also allows us to see the new types of industrial agglomerations forming in the backward districts.

LOCATION PROCESS OF AUTOMOBILE MANUFACTURERS AND RELATED INDUSTRIES

For our next analysis, we will look at the automobile and related industries which are representative of Pithampur. By understanding their production activities we will try to understand the characteristics of industrial agglomeration. For the sake of convenience, here we classify automobile and two-wheeler assembly factories into A group, automobile related factories in the 1996 survey in B group, and surveyed factories from 1990 into C group. We assigne sequential numbers to each of these according to the date of establishment, older factories first (see Table 9.2 and Figure 9.1). For our analysis, the main subject is on groups A and B; C group is considered complementarily.

Table 9.2: Outline of surveyed automobile and related factories

No.	*Year of establishment*	*Fixed capital (Rs. in lakhs)*	*Products*	*Origin*	*Employment*
A-1	1984	17,902	Car engine	Kolkata	447
A-2	1986	*1,692	Scooter	Pune	1,405
A-3	1986	*2,892	Light commercial vehicle	Faridabad	780
A-4	1987	*1,361	Light commercial vehicle	Pune	900
B-1	1983	524	Camshafts castings	Delhi	63
B-2	1986	1,000	Plastic scooter parts	Mumbai	105
B-3	1987	25	Bus body building	Indore	50
B-4	1991	300	Bus body building	Faridabad	30
B-5	1992	225	Bus body building	Indore	172
B-6	1992	100	Wheel hubs	Pithampur	21
B-7	1993	12	Sheet metal	Pune	19
B-8	1996	n.a.	Two wheeler parts	Ludhiana	48
B-9	1996	45	Body building	Pune	22
B-10	1996	20	Automobile seats	Pune	11
C-1	1986	*35	Sheet metal	Delhi	*25
C-2	1986	*262	Aluminium die casting	Indore	*90
C-3	1986	n.a.	Sheet metal	Indore	n.a.
C-4	1987	*60	Cargo body	Indore	*60
C-5	1988	*21	Press parts	Pune	*37
C-6	1989	*113	Sheet metal	Ludhiana	*88

Note: C-3 was closed in 1996.
Source: Interview survey in 1995 and 1996.
* From industrial data of AKVN (Indore).

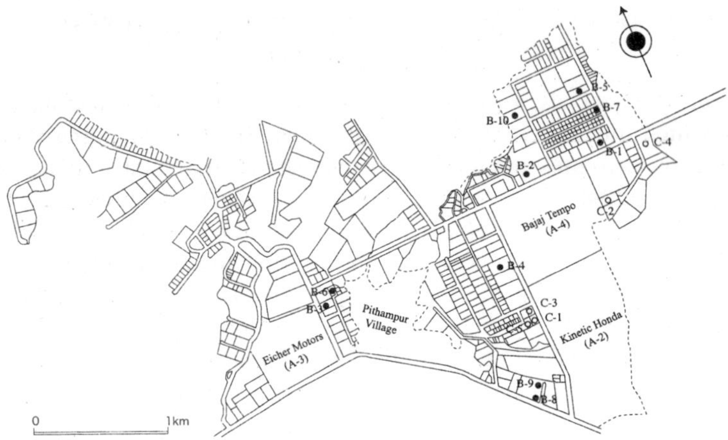

Figure 9.1: Distribution of surveyed factories in Pithampur, Sectors 1 and 2

Automobile Manufacturers

Four automobile and two-wheeler manufacturers have moved into Pithampur and form the core of the industrial agglomeration here. Below is an overview of each of these manufacturers.

A-1 is Hindustan Motors Limited (HML). This company is based in Kolkata, but due frequent labour disputes interfering with operations there, it has adopted a strategy of spreading factories in various regions. Its passenger car engine and transmission departments began production in 1984 in Pithampur's Sector 3, and from 1998 it began production of multipurpose vehicles for rural use.

A-2 Kinetic Honda (KH), was a joint venture corporation between Japan's Honda and the Kinetic Group, a midsized conglomerate in India. The venture was dissolved in 1998; Honda relinquished management control and the name was changed, but in this discussion the name of the company at the time of the survey will be used. The Kinetic Group is made up of three companies: KH, Bajaj Tempo (BT) and Kinetic Engineering (KE). The head office of all three companies is located in Pune, and except for KE the factories are located here, and together the group has been one of the largest contributors to Pithampur's growth.

KH was founded in 1984 and began production in 1986. At first, Honda only held 28.6 per cent of stock, but with deregulation of foreign investment, it acquired management control though a majority stock purchase of 50.9 per cent. However, as mentioned above, it subsequently surrendered the management of the company. KH produces 100cc scooters. Privately owned Bajaj Auto dominates India's scooter market, and in 1996 commanded a majority share of domestic production (1.32 million units). KH is in fourth place with an 8.4 per cent share, but its innovative product designs are popular among the younger generation.

A-3 is Eicher Motors (EM), a business belonging to the Eicher Group (based in Delhi) and famous for its tractor production. Fifteen per cent of its shares are owned by Japan's Mitsubishi Group. When it began production in 1986, it produced Mitsubishi's Canter truck under a technical tie-up, but since Mitsubishi dissolved the collaborative agreement and pulled out its Japanese advisers at the beginning of the 1990s, EM has run its operations independently since 1994. Its yearly production in 1996 was 6,500 units and was in third place (4.4 per cent) in the domestic small commercial vehicle market.

A-4 is Bajaj Tempo (BT), which has a technical tie-up with Germany's Daimler Benz for small commercial vehicles and engines, and began operations in 1987. Its products are Jeep style vehicles and small commercial vehicles. Its main product, the Matador, is an especially well-known vehicle. It is in second place after TELCO (now Tata Motors) in the small commercial vehicle market with an 18 per cent market share (1996).

These four companies' primary decision to move into Pithampur was government assistance and aid. By moving here, these companies were eligible for generous financial support and preferential tax treatment. Another reason was the ability to acquire large land tracts, but KH said it was drawn by the plentiful labour force. This was due to KH's relatively unskilled labour force, and because its labour supply/demand mechanism was different from that of the other automakers.

Automobile Related Industries

Next, the amount of capital investment and the number of employees for factories in the B group, we investigate the characteristics of the automobile related industries. The average capital investment was Rs. 20 million. About 50-60 employees were average, and only two factories—B-2 and B-5—had more than 100 employees. This indicates the relatively small-scale makeup of the group.

Businesses of these factories can be largely separated into automobile body construction and component manufacturing. Automobile body construction refers to the process of attaching the vehicle body to the platform manufactured by the automaker. The same platform is used for truck and bus assembly, but the body construction of buses is frequently outsourced. Reasons for this include simplification of the automaker's production line, and ability to offset labour costs to sub-contractors by outsourcing manpower-intensive assembly processes. Three surveyed factories fall into this automobile body construction category. Coinciding with EM's move to Pithampur, B-3 and B-5 were set up as subsidiaries in Pithampur by the owners who had performed automobile body construction in Indore. B-9 is owned by its parent company in Pune, and because of the growth in automobile demand in recent years it decided to build a new factory, and moved to Pithampur in 1996.

Next, we will look at component factories. B-1 is a joint venture between an Indian industrialist and a German firm. It began operations in 1983 and is renowned for its technical prowess in producing engine camshafts. B-2 is the main factory for a company headquartered in Mumbai. It began production in 1986; its main product is plastic components. B-4 is the manufacturing arm of a firm headquartered in Faridabad, and produces cabins for a tractor maker located in Pithampur Sector 3. B-6 is a business launched in 1992 by its owner who left a Japanese firm. It manufactures various types of wheel hubs. B-7 is the subsidiary of a Pune based firm. Producing sheet metal components and performing simple assembly operations. B-8 is the subsidiary founded in 1996 by company C-6 from Sector 3, and manufactures pressed components for scooters. B-10 manufactures automobile seats, and began production in 1996. The owner of this firm is the son-in-law of the head of the Kinetic Group; this firm can be considered to be a member of the same group.

Of the surveyed automotive component factories, the head offices or parent companies of five were in Maharashtra, three in the northern states of India, and only two factories were started by local Indore business people. For the C group, approximately half of the firms were local and the other half from other states. When asked the most important reason for choosing Pithampur, six factories said 'the presence of an automaker with which we do business'. If we include factories which gave this as the second and third reasons, excepting B-1 which does not have existing business ties with other companies here, nine factories emphasised this. During the 1990 survey, all surveyed firms cited the presence of an automobile maker with which they have business ties as the number one reason for moving here.

The agglomeration of automotive-related industries at Pithampur was brought on by the arrival of the four automakers, who were attracted there by large subsidies from the government. A secondary factor in the formation of this agglomeration was that existing component manufacturers had set up subsidiaries or branch factories here, away from the core automobile industry regions of Maharastra and northern India. Also, some local automotive-industry related business people around Indore and some entrepreneurs with engineering skills took this chance to set up factories in Pithampur and expand their production to meet the needs of the automakers. In this way, automotive industry agglomeration at Pithampur is considered to be the result of automobile related factories moving here due to the presence of four automobile manufacturers and their growth in production.

PRODUCTION LINKAGES BETWEEN AUTOMOBILE MANUFACTURERS AND RELATED INDUSTRIES

Automobile Manufacturers' Trade Structure

Of the four automobile/two-wheeled vehicle companies, the locations of component suppliers for HML and KH are clear (see Table 9.3). HML buys 747 different components from 130 vendors. KH buys 844 different components from 136 vendors. HML's Pithampur business is engine and transmission assembly, so the parts suppliers it deals with are naturally different from those used by KH, which builds scooters. However, when looking at the location of the suppliers of these two companies, we find very strong similarities.

Both companies have close relations with western India including Maharashtra and Gujarat, which are home to majority of component manufactures for both companies. They also acquire components from all across India, with several suppliers based in northern India mainly around Delhi, and southern India centred around Chennai. This is the spatial characteristic of the components' trade. When taking transportation costs into consideration, acquiring components close to the assembly factory will reduce overall manufacturing cost. However, industrialisation in MP was lagging, companies that manufacturing automotive components were few, and there was a limit to the number of parts that automakers could procure from within the state. This was one factor that led to business relations with other states.

Table 9.3: Location of suppliers for Hindustan Motors and Kinetic Honda

Region	Hindustan Motors		Kinetic Honda	
	No. of suppliers	No. of items	No. of suppliers	No. of items
North	20 (15.4)	167 (22.4)	16 (11.8)	109 (12.9)
West	67 (51.5)	397 (53.1)	77 (56.6)	375 (44.4)
East	3 (2.3)	23 (3.1)	–	–
South	27 (20.8)	96 (12.9)	16 (11.8)	99 (11.7)
Central	13 (10.0)	64 (8.6)	23 (16.9)	243 (28.8)
Unidentified	–	–	4 (2.9)	13 (1.5)
Total	130 (100.0)	747 (100.0)	136 (100.0)	844 (100.0)

Note: North: Delhi, Haryana, Panjab, Uttar Pradesh;
West: Maharashtra, Gujarat;
East: West Bengal, Orissa, Bihar;
South: Karnataka, Andhra Pradesh, Kerala, Tamil Nadu.

Source: Interviewed from both companies.

For both companies, we would consider the most important factor in the formation of business ties with western India. For KH, a big reason was the operations of the Kinetic Group, the company's parent, based in Pune. The company has close relations with component manufacturers in Maharashtra around Pune, and procures parts from them. For KH, this could be interpreted as evidence that the group has strong relations in its home region.

On the other hand, instead of eastern India where its headquarters is located, HML's Pithampur factory has strong business ties with component factories in western India. The reason for this becomes clear when we look at the component trade makeup of HML. According to the *Buyer's Guide* published by the Automobile Component Manufacturers Association of India, 108 firms have direct trade with HML. Of their factory locations, 35 are in western India, 31 are in the south, 27 are in the north, but only 11 in the east. This shows that HML overall depends on components supplied from existing automobile industry agglomerations in India, not from the region of its headquarters in Kolkata. This overall trade makeup of HML is reflected also in parts procurement at its Pithampur factory, and can be viewed as being centred around western India.

When we look at trade partners in the home region of MP, for KH, the percentage was slightly higher at 17 per cent. Also, it procured approximately 30 per cent of all its parts from its home state. As mentioned above, when KH moved into Pithampur, 14 component companies decided to follow KH there, expecting increases in orders. HML, on the other hand, only located its engine and transmission operations here, and did not move its vehicle assembly process. In addition, as can be seen from the relatively small production volume in HML, component manufacturers were not tempted to move here. The above factors were responsible for the differences between these firms in the numbers of procurement partners located in MP.

Trade Structure of Automobile Related Industries

From the automobile makers' perspective, most component suppliers are located in other states, and procurement from within the state has been limited. Even so, about 50 Pithampur factories can be classified as automobile related industries, and an understanding of their production relationships is key to understanding the qualities of this industrial agglomeration. Figure 9.2 arranges trade partners from the perspective of automotive related factories surveyed, and in terms of trade value, it shows for the top two trade partners as well as name of delivery recipient and location.

First, we shall look at vehicle body construction manufacturers. Companies B-3 and B-5 transport platforms manufactured by EM to their own factories, assemble with bus bodies, and ship them back to EM after painting. A production relationship with piece work characteristics is formed with automobile manufacturers. B-9 buys multipurpose vehicle frames from BT and sends to a dealer in Bhopal after adding bodies and completing the vehicle. This is due to BT's production sales strategy;

Vendors				Custormers		
India	MP	Pithampur	Units	Pithampur	MP	India
◎(MS)	◎(Gwalior)		B-1			MUL(HY)
◎◎(MS)			B-2	KH, EM		
		•EM	B-3	EM		
◎(MS),◎(RS)			B-4	L&T		
		•EM	B-5	EM		
	○(Indore)	○	B-6	EM	GG(Dewas)	
	◎◎(Indore)		B-7	BT		BT(MS)
◎(PJ)	◎(Indore)		B-8	KH		
		•BT	B-9		□(Bhopal)	
◎◎(AP)			B-10	BT		

Type of trade: ◎purchase, ○job work, •body construction, □dealer
States: PJ: Punjab, MS: Maharashtra, RS: Rajastan, AP: Andhra Pradesh, HY: Haryana
Manufacturers: KH; Kinetic Honda, L&T: Larson & Tarbo, BT: Bajaj Tempo, EM: Eicher Motors, GG: Gajra Gears, MUL; Maruti Udyog

Figure 9.2: Production linkage of the automobile related factories in Pithampur

other than this, the two factories mentioned above are essentially identical.

We explain the remaining 7 factories. First, trade within Pithampur can be said to be sparse. The only notable case is B-6 which outsources its contracted labour operations through job work; for other surveyed factories, raw materials and semi-finished products procured from outside Pithampur Industrial Growth Centre. The nearest vendors are in Indore (three in all). From outside the state, there are strong ties with firms in Maharashtra (four in all). For customers, automobile and tractor makers within Pithampur are important, and except for B-1, nine factories have trade relations with at least one of these manufacturers. The distribution for customers is limited mainly to Pithampur, providing insight into the close relationships and factories' reasons for moving to this location as mentioned earlier. Only the three companies B-1, B-6, and B-7 have trade with manufacturers outside Pithampur.

The production relationship of automobile and related industries in Pithampur can be summarised as follows. Automobile and two-wheeled vehicle manufacturers located here have trade ties with component companies in western India, and the relationship with existing core automotive manufacturing regions is considered strong. Only 10-20 per cent of overall trade ties for Pithampur factories are with companies from within the state, and furthermore most of these are with factories that relocated here from existing industrial centres. With one exception, as a general rule, automobile related industries situated here have Pithampur automakers as their customers and maintain close relationships with them. However, the out-of-state ratio is higher for procurement of raw materials and semi-finished goods, for which there are no relationships were with factories in Pithampur.

CHARACTERISTICS OF INDUSTRIAL AGGLOMERATION AT PITHAMPUR

Industrial development in Pithampur began in 1983 and as of 1995, 335 factories were in operation employing approximately 25,000 people, making this the largest industrial agglomeration in MP. The enactment of various preferential policies by the government, and its location at the edge of Indore, the largest business city in the region, are behind the large number of factories coming to Pithampur. Factories moving here are mainly in modern industries and have a nationwide target market, and greatly differ from the typical industry of MP until now, whose business tended to target the local market. There is especially a trend of automobile and related industries locating here, and Pithampur has become one of the largest agglomerations of the automobile industry in industrial growth centres developed in India's backward districts.

However, our discussion has shown that Pithampur is still a developing industrial agglomeration in terms of production relationships. The business partners for automotive related factories were entirely automobile manufacturers which located here. Their presence has contributed greatly to the development of Pithampur. However, from the perspective of automakers, parts procurement activities from within Pithampur are still at a low level and dependence on places like Mumbai and Pune is still extremely high. The weak manufacturing relationship with the local region is a notable characteristic of industrial agglomerations in backward districts. This will be clearer after the comparison with NOIDA and Greater NOIDA regions, which are discussed in Chapter 15.

CHAPTER 10

Characteristics of the Industrial Labour Market

HIDENORI OKAHASHI

CHARACTERISTICS OF THE LABOUR MARKET IN INDIA

For long, India has struggled with unemployment and labour issues. Labour is classified into two categories: organised labour (all offices belonging to the public sector, and offices in the private sector with more than 25 employees) and unorganised labour (farmers, farm labourers, and settlement and domestic workers). A staggering majority of workers toil in the unorganised sector under inferior labour conditions, and employment in the organised sector is extremely rare. Similar to most developing nations, India's labour market can be characterised as having a segmented structure and predominantly unorganised labour market.

What changes will the rapid progress of industrialisation in modern India bring to this labour market? Until now, a detailed attempt to understand the state of the industrial labour market has not been done.

In this chapter, we reveal traits of the labour market for Pithampur Industrial Growth Centre from two perspectives: workers in two large scale automobile manufacturing factories, and workers seeking temporary employment in the industrial estate. Kinetic Honda (KH) and Eicher Motors (EM) have been taken up as large-scale factory case studies.

LABOUR MARKET FOR LARGE FACTORIES—CASE STUDIES

Labour Makeup for the Factories

An overview of EM and KH factories was provided in the previous chapter. Here we will discuss only their labour makeup (see Table 10.1). Permanent employees can be separated into three categories: executives ranking manager or higher, staffs such as technicians and office workers,

Table 10.1: Outline of surveyed factories and respondents

		Keinetic Honda	Eicher Motors
Founded in		1984	1986
Starting-up year of the Pithampur factory		1986	1986
Main products		Scooter	Light commercial vehicle
Location of the main office		Pune (Maharashtra)	Indore (Madhya Pradesh)
No. of employees in 1995	Total	1,534	818
	Executive	45	129
	Staff	346	386
	Permanent workers	674	303
	Temporary workers	469	0
No. of employees in 1990	Total	1,295	407
	Exective	33	59
	Staff	275	201
	Permanent workers	680	147
	Temporary workers	307	0
Interviewed employees in 1990	Total	85	87
	Staff	39	37
	Workers	46	50

Note: Interview survey was held at each factory in October, 1990.
Source: Campany data.

and workers directly involved in the manufacturing process. Frequently temporary workers are employed, though the number differs from factory to factory. Additionally, not included in employee numbers are day workers employed in such tasks as component shipping or factory cleaning. However, it is common for these workers to be contract workers.

The survey was dome on 85 KH and 87 EM workers. Since executives were excluded from this study, only staff and workers comprised the sample. All were men, and nearly all were in their 20s or 30s. For KH, those in their 20s were 67 per cent by the sample, and those in their 30s were 29 per cent. For EM the corresponding figures were 63 per cent and 33 per cent. This tendency toward young workers reflects the relatively young state of operations of these factories.

KH, three of four employees were from non-administrative departments; this low ratio of administrative employees is notable. In 1995, only 3 per cent were executives, 23 per cent were staff, and these two together accounted for only one administrative employee for four non-administrative employees. Only for 1 of 4 employees. KH had a large number of temporary workers, exceeding 30 per cent of the entire work force. And this ratio has been increasing in recent years. This is the due to KH's relatively high demand for unskilled labour. Also, learning from its experience decrease production in 1992 and 1993, it uses temporary workers as an economic safety valve. Since laying off full-time employees is legally extremely difficult in India, this strategy to hire temporary workers for short periods is frequently used.

For EM, on the other hand, administrative executive and staff employees formed over half of the employees, their numbers significantly greater than non-administrative employees. In 1995, 17 per cent were executives and 23 per cent were staff, adding up to as much as 64 per cent of the total, with workers being only 36 per cent. Also, because the manufacturing process requires skilled labour, temporary workers were not employed. To secure skilled engineers and skilled labour for the initial factory launch, about 60 people were relocated from the EM group's Eicher Tractor Corporation. Wages at this factory were among the highest at Pithampur, and worker turnover was low.

Labour Force Supply Area

Where does a large factory situated in a backward district like Pithampur obtain its workforce? We try to understand the labour force supply area by studying the previous living area and job.

Let us look at the place of living in the previous job, in other words the previous residence. Workers who had previously lived elsewhere in MP or who did not move at all, the so-called 'original MP residents' in KH were 66 per cent and 47 per cent in EM. KH's in-state workers were slightly higher, but half were hired from KH's home state. For both companies, the ratio of original MP residents was higher for workers than for staff. Outside of MP, for KH only Maharashtra stood out, but for EM, relocations from Haryana amounted to as high as 20 per cent. This was due to the large number of employees transfered from EM's tractor factory in Haryana. When looking only at worker migration within MP, KH workers were more wide ranging than workers from EM. Other than each of the surrounding five districts which accounted for about 10 per cent, KH's labour force was widely distributed across MP.

For both firms there were many workers who changed their professions, but few who were previously self-employed farm workers or day labourers. Most new hires were previously employed in factories as workers or staff, or had non-manufacturing industry backgrounds such as office work or technical services.

When looking at the relation of previous residence to previous job, for both companies the neighbouring large city of Indore was a large labour supply source of those leaving previous jobs in factories or companies, accounting for about 30 per cent of labourers. Additionally, KH recruited from factories in neighbouring industrial areas. On the other hand, both companies only hired one or two individuals from nearby Dhar, another industrially backward district.

Thus, the labour market for permanent employees for the two companies covered all of India; at the same time, city Indore and its surrounding industrial areas have played an important role in providing employees. Very few employees had been hired from the district of Dhar. Dependence on MP state was higher for recruiting workers than for staff.

Differences between the two companies are: KH depended on local labour, gathering its workforce from a wide area of western MP including Indore. Many workers had been hired from nearby local companies. EM transfered in many of its workers from its operations in other states, and even for 'worker' jobs, its dependence on MP was low and its labour came from all over the country including south India.

Hiring Methods and Means of Participation for Candidates

KH recruited staff and exectives through newspaper advertisements, and made hiring decisions based on documentary elimination and candidate interviews. While workers were also recruited through newspaper advertisements, some candidates directly visited the factory or a friend or acquaintance. As will be discussed later, people directly visiting the factory were hired according to the same method used for hiring temporary workers. From the company's perspective this process allowed it to simplify the hiring process. This highlights the significance of an informal network in hiring decisions. But workers hired in this way, were seen as obedient but lacking in motivation.

Unlike KH, EM recruited staff and workers mainly from within MP through newspaper advertisements, and made its hiring decisions based on document screening and candidate interviews. Furthermore, HR representatives visited colleges and held campus interviews to recruit the best graduates. The company regarded its workers as obedient and able to endure hard work, with a low turnover rate. The problem was at the staff level. As many staff members from south India and other distant regions who joined the factory when it was first launched left, the company decided to hire locally whenever possible. Compared to workers, it is common in India for staff and higher employees to move between companies, but for this kind of backward district lacking urban conveniences, securing workers becomes an even more difficult task.

From the above, we see that employee hiring methods can be formal such as newspaper advertisements and campus interviews, and also informal such as direct visits to the factory by candidates, and introductions by friends or acquaintances who are current employees. This shows that behind the excess supply of workers, a labour market environment is forming which has imperfect competition characteristics. However, for staff and higher, the conditions are slightly different. The factories are faced with difficulties in attracting and keeping skilled resources due to the regional issues intrinsic to backward districts, and for this reason formal hiring methods are common.

Labour Supply: Social Background

Let us look at the social attributes of the labour market in terms of educational level and caste. First, the educational system of MP is as follows. Students first attend five years of elementary school, then three years of junior school or five years of high school. For post-secondary education there is two years of higher secondary school, and above that, for Industrial Training Institute (ITI) or higher education there are three-year colleges and graduate schools.

In KH, 50 per cent of staff were college graduates. 20 per cent were as graduate school alumni, and in addition to high school or higher secondary schools, a respectable number had completed ITI. A handful of workers had only completed middle school, but most were high school or higher secondary school graduates, and some of them had graduated from ITIs as well.

Of the EM staff, half were college graduates and 37.8 per cent were school graduates; together they made up 90 per cent of the staff, notable for its extremely high educational level. While approximately 30 per cent of workers were middle school or high school graduates, there was high educational level here as well, with more than half having graduated from high school or higher secondary school and gone on to do an ITI course.

Among the newly hired workers, the lowest educational level in both companies was higher secondary school. Workers who were ITI graduates with certain specialised skills were preferred. The educational level of staff was higher in EM than KH, as the former bad administration and product development departments.

Table 10.2 shows the relationship between employees' caste and religion and their Job status. Caste grouping is based on Varna, and Hindus are separated into Brahmins as the highest class, Kshatriya as other upper classes, Vaishya and Shudra as middle classes, and Scheduled Castes and Scheduled Tribes receiving policy protection as the lowest classes.

In both companies, the Brahmins and other upper castes made up the largest percentages. There are a few members of lower castes, and even these few were found among the workers. More staff were members of higher castes than workers; 'Brahmin' were the most prevalent, though there are Christians, Jains and other non-Hindus in addition to members of other higher castes. Most workers were from other upper castes than Brahmin. A little less than 20 per cent were from middle castes, but even in this group, there were only a few from the lower castes.

When we look at father's occupation, 30-40 per cent self-employed farmers, while it is notable that public workers, teachers, office workers and administrators added upto around 50 per cent of the total. Thus, there was a move in the previous generation itself toward non-agricultural professions, and the earning power appears to have enabled offspring to obtain better education, which in turn made possible employment in high-level professions. When looking at father's profession and caste, while self-employed farmers did not tend to belong to any one caste, public workers, as well as company workers and administrators, tended to be belonging to Brahmin or other upper castes.

Based on this, we think the tendency for employees to borne into upper castes is due to the educational requirements of better jobs, and obtaining this education is closely related to the social standing and earning power of one's parents. Also, informal means of gaining employment in an over-supplied labour market through friends or acquaintances plays an important role, thought to have a positive effect on factory employment for members of castes already represented at the factory.

Table 10.2: Distribution of interviwed employees by caste/community

Campany	*Employment status*	*Upper-level caste*		*Middle-level caste*	*Lower-level caste*	*non Hindhu religiou group*	*nonresponse not classificabl*	*Total*
		Brahman	*Other jati*					
	Staff	15	14	1	0	5	4	39
		38.5	35.9	2.6	0.0	12.8	10.3	100%
		12	14	8	3	8	1	46
Keinetic Honda	Worker	26.1	30.4	17.4	6.5	17.4	2.2	100%
	Total	27	28	9	3	13	5	85
		31.8	32.9	10.6	3.5	15.3	5.9	100%
	Staff	13	9	0	0	8	7	37
		35.1	24.3	0.0	0.0	21.6	18.9	100%
Eicher Motors	Worker	8	17	8	2	7	8	50
		16.0	34.0	16.0	4.0	14.0	16.0	100%
	Total	21	26	8	2	15	15	87
		24.1	29.9	9.2	2.3	17.2	17.2	100%

Note: Caste classification is as follows. Upper-level caste: Brahmin and Kshatriya, Middle-level caste: Vaishya and Shudra, Lower-level caste: SC and ST
Source: Interview survey in October 1990.

Table 10.3: Caste/community and father's occupation of job-seekers

	Cultivator	*Small manufacturing*	*Agricultural/ General labour*	*Factory worker*	*Clerk/ Engineer*	*Civil servant*	*Teacher*	*Shopowner*	*Total*	*%*
Upper-level caste (Brahman)	0	0	0	1	0	0	0	0	1	1.7
Upper-level caste (except Brahman)	9	1	0	0	2	2	0	0	14	23.3
Middle-level caste	15	0	2	0	1	3	1	0	22	36.7
Lower-level caste (SC)	5	0	0	0	0	1	2	0	8	13.3
Lower-level caste (ST)	6	0	1	0	0	0	0	0	7	11.7
Muslim	0	0	0	0	0	0	0	1	1	1.7
nonresponse/not classificable	4	0	0	1	2	0	0	0	7	11.7
Total (actual number)	39	1	3	2	5	6	3	1	60	100.0
Percentage (%)	65.0	1.7	5.0	3.3	8.3	10.0	5.0	1.7	100.0	

Source: Interview survey in November 1996.

STRUCTURE OF THE TEMPORARY WORKER LABOUR MARKET

Composition of Job Seekers

People seeking work can be found in front of factory gates inside Pithampur Industrial Growth Centre. To understand the status of job seekers, we interviewed some individualy waiting in front of KH's main gate.

Most were young and unmarried; almost 77 per cent were those between 19 and 23 years old. An overwhelming 80 per cent were unmarried. They were attempting to participate in Pithampur's labour market based on information obtained informally. Almost 60 per cent said they came here based on 'information from a friend'; 30 per cent said they came based on 'information from a family member' or 'information from a relative'.

These job seekers can be largely separated into two types. The first of these were individuals who had previously worked at Pithampur; the second were individuals visiting Pithampur for the first time. Interesting here is that the all of the former group were individuals who had been employed in the past as temporary workers. Temporary work was offered for a periods of five months, and if not renewed the workers were laid off. More job seekers were seen in front of KH than any other factory in Pithampur because of its extremely high dependence on temporary labourers. The wages of these individuals were the lowest for males in unskilled manufacturing in the state.

Home Regions of Job Seekers and Social Characteristics

Three of four job seekers coming to Pithampur lived within MP, and the remaining 25 per cent were from outside MP. Of the other states, other than Maharashtra which is closest accounted for the half of the job seekers, with a few coming from other neighbouring states of UP, Bihar and Orissa. Of those from MP, many came from districts neighbouring Dhar, in which Pithampur is located; job seekers also came from distant regions such as the northeast, showing that the area supplying temporary labour force was very wide.

Seventy per cent of those seeking temporary work had no previous experience, emphasising that this labour market consisted mainly of new graduates. On the other hand, a relatively large 15 per cent of this group came from an agricultural background, showing that it had the characteristic of attracting rural unemployed. All the job seekers had middle school or higher education, but there were many–almost 60 per cent–who had completed high school or higher secondary school. Nearly 10 per cent had finished college or graduate school, and 20 per cent had completed ITI training. Compared to permanent workers, temporary workers were less educated such as high school graduates, but the difference was not great.

Regarding caste, more than half were from the middle castes as well as Scheduled Castes or Scheduled Tribes (see Table 10.3). There was only 1 Brahmin and 14 from other upper castes, and together they only made up 25 per cent of the total; compared to the permanent employees mentioned earlier, the number of upper caste individuals bere is significantly lower. For nearly 70 per cent, their father's profession was agriculture, differing greatly from the results of permanent workers.

Temporary Labour Market Characteristics

Temporary labour did not pay well, and workers were subject to uncertainty of the possibility of being easily laid off at the end of the five month contracted employment period. However, the working conditions at a large-scale factory at Pithampur were better than small- and medium-scale factories in surrounding areas, and there remained a slim possibility of becoming a permanent employee. For this reason the labour market covered a large area including MP and neighbouring states, and also has the characteristic of encompassing not only new graduates but also agricultural workers and the large labour reservoir in rural populations.

There were many from extremely low levels of society, especially the Scheduled Castes and Scheduled Tribes. Most of workers had completed middle school, but a few had also had specialised job training. Many were the offsprings of farmers, and for this reason it is thought that there were many who lacked access to informal networks for finding employment opportunities.

CHARACTERISTICS OF THE LARGE-SCALE LABOUR MARKET IN BACKWARD DISTRICTS

The labour market model for large-scale factories at Pithampur is shown in Figure 10.1. Roughly three levels of labour markets can be identified; among permanent employees, two labour markets for staff and higher and workers can be seen. Furthermore, there is a labour market for temporarary workers below these.

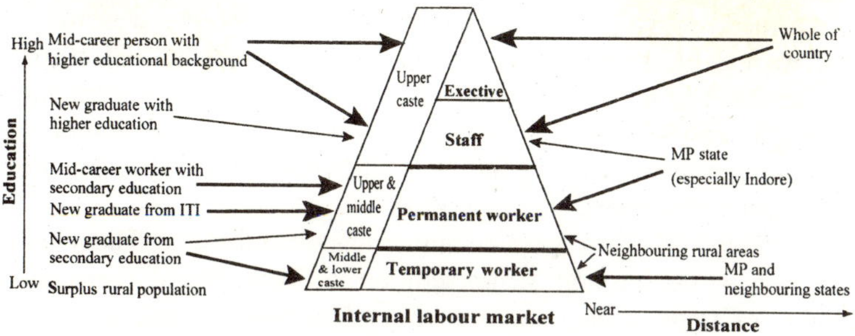

Figure 10.1: Labour market of large-scale factories in Pithampur Industrial Growth Centre

These three labour markets differ on both source of workforce and supply area. First, for the workforce source, educational level is critical. There are large differences in workforce demand for those completing higher education, those completing middle school education and having technical education, and middle school graduates. In relation to previous employment, members of the staff and workers labour market are typically skilled labourers with previous experience or new graduates. A characteristic of the temporary labour force is that in addition to new graduates, it includes people from rural areas with agricultural experience. The work conditions for the temporary labour market at Pithampur are unstable, but since they are still favourable compared to agriculture or other work in villages, they attract underutilised young workers from rural areas. In this way, even for recently developed industrial areas, we can observe the formation of labour markets already divided as seen above.

Differences in the workforce supply area are also evident for each labour market. While staff and higher employees come from all over India, permanent and temporary workers are mainly from MP. In MP, where Pithampur is situated, there is excess supply of unskilled labour force like workers Thus, it is very easy to attract workers, but on the other hand it is difficult to attract and retain valuable employees in the staff or higher level, which demands higher education and greater skills.

Of course, because the workforce demanded by each of this labour market differs, differences are seen in the hiring methods for these employees. Formal methods such as newspaper advertisements are common for staff and executives, but for permanent workers, in addition to formal methods such as newspaper advertisements and campus visits, informal methods such as introductions by current employees play an important role. Furthermore temporary workers are selected from job seekers gathered factory gates looking for work based on information from friends or acquaintances. These conditions are a reflection of the disproportionate labour supply for the available demand, a labour market environment with imperfect competition.

In India, a link exists between labour market and castes. The permanent labour market for large-scale factories of this study is dominated by Brahmin and upper castes; there are very few from the middle castes, and virtually no members of lower castes. Furthermore, there was a tendency for staff more than workers to belong to upper castes. On the other hand, the lower Scheduled Castes and Scheduled Tribes stood out among those seeking temporary work.

This kind of interplay between castes and job types is not limited to the fields of this case study. However, it is difficult to determine whether this caste bias for workers is the result of caste-based discrimination. We can only say that each job requires a certain educational level, and education depends on parents' occupation; in other words it corresponds closely to the earning power of one's parents. Actually, the father's occupation allows us to see clear differences in caste. Furthermore, in over-supplied labour markets, the role of informal participation through friends and acquaintances is great, and this is thought to present favourable conditions for individuals whose caste members are already working at these factories.

From this logic, increases in educational level bring the possibility of change. Related to this, it is important to note that in India, since its independence, special affirmative action programme have been carried out to erase social and economic disadvantages for lower castes (Scheduled Castes and Scheduled Tribes). Reserving seats in higher education, public sector employment, and legislative are examples of these reservation policies, but together with scholarship programs, they are contributing to increase education level.

Finally, while Pithampur is part of the 'Tribal Belt,' a region with many Scheduled Tribes, it is worth noting that industrial development has not lead to better conditions for these tribes. This was also noted by Purohit[1] and Thakur and Thakur,[2] and is one problem in industrialisation in backward districts with many Scheduled Tribes. The reasons for that are the obvious low earning power of Scheduled Tribes and low education level. To alleviate this, setting up ITI for tribes inside industrial estates is a challenge. But corporations have failed to set up facilities to teach technical skills needed for the workers they need to hire. On this point, Thakur and Thakur[3] also assert that unemployment of ITI graduates in industrial estates goes together with a skilled labour force shortage, and they recommend that firms located here take responsibility for building and running ITIs. Weak infrastructure is already cited as a bottleneck for industrialisation in India, but for the future, there should also be close consideration of incomplete development of human resources.

NOTES

1 Y.S. Purohit, *Industrialising Economy and Labour Market*, New Delhi: Mittal Publications, 1989.
2 D. Thakur and D.N. Thakur, *Industrialisation in Tribal Areas*, New Delhi: Deep & Deep Publications, 1994.
3 Ibid., p. 363.

CHAPTER 11

Housing Colony Residents and Lifestyle

YOSHIMICHI YUI

HOUSING PROBLEM IN INDIA

In India, policies have been made to resolve housing problems, and an Indian-style housing system has been developed based on these policies. However, this system varies by region, and laws defining these housing policies change constantly, complicating the housing supply situation.[1] This is because in India, housing policy falls under jurisdiction of the states, and each state or regional municipality handles this differently. For this reason, when examining housing issues in India, it is necessary to look from a regional perspective.

In India's emerging industrial cities, large-scale housing is being provided, with single-family homes and low-rise apartments emerging. This kind of housing development developed together with industrial areas has functioned as place of residence for the first labourers living in company housing for new companies or in public housing. Here, we would like to focus on housing development that follows industrialisation.

In this chapter, using the example of industrial estates in backward districts, we consider the planning and current state of housing supply following industrial development. And by understanding resident qualities, we also consider the role of the urban manager in forming resident groups.

THE HOUSING SUPPLY SYSTEM IN INDIA

According to Bose,[2] in India, in addition to building houses for higher incomes, it was thought that people would build homes only after reaching a certain age. Housing demand was low, and it was extremely unusual for a young head of a household to build or look for a house early in his career. Also, the loan systems needed for private home construction were incomplete, and there were many procedural difficulties.

However, this mentality has been changing in recent years. More than before, house building through large capital outlays is decreasing. Housing demand has strengthened because it has become easier to build and buy homes at reasonable prices. Also, families are beginning to demand improved living quarters, and consumption trends following increases in income are also being directed toward housing.

In India, the Development Authority handles land development and infrastructure, while the Housing Board oversees housing construction. Because the land provision and housing construction are overseen by two different organisations, a large gap has formed between urban planning and housing supply. Also, because there are high road or rail transportation costs involved in living in areas surrounding metropolitan areas, developments have benefitted the wealthy classes more than the poorer classes.

The housing supply in India is divided into the housing market funded through private capital and the public housing market, with direct involvement of the government. Pugh[3] categorised this housing supply structure into; a housing market triggered by capital for high-income or middle-income earners; a public housing market for low-income households; and shelters used by low-income slum dwellers or street dwellers.

The main supplier of public housing is generally the Housing Board of each state. A national standard exists for supplied housing: HIG for high-income group, MIG for middle-income group, LIG for low-income group, and EWS for the very low-income economically weaker section. MP in the year 1996, the yearly income level for each group was Rs. 1,25,000 and higher for HIG, Rs. 1,00,000-1,25,000 for MIG, Rs. 24,000-1,00,000 for LIG, and Rs. 24,000 or less for EWS.

The layout for each of these dwellings was living room bedrooms and kitchen and a combined shower and toilet, but by additional construction on open spaces around the entrance and adding a room on the second floor, the actual living spaces vary and external appearances differ. By allowing housing improvements by the owner, the housing suppliers have been able to implement 'low cost housing,' and while this allows for a housing supply that meets the lifestyle of the residents, it also keeps construction costs down, in line with the objective of the housing suppliers.

Open spaces are also emphasised from the point of forming rurban communities (urban/rural combined communities) in urban and regional planning in India.[4] Aiming to combine seemingly contradictory urban and rural characteristics, an open space has been planned in front of each dwelling to realise this kind of community. Even in modern housing which tends to respect privacy, by providing a place for preparing food with neighbours like in rural areas or for engaging in neighbourhood gossip, it provides a stage for various communications between residents, and allows social interaction.

HOUSING COLONY DEVELOPMENT

At Pithampur Industrial Growth Centre, planned in a rural area, provision of housing to secure a workforce was an immediate concern, and a residential estate was built. Housing within the colony was intended for families, and encouraged workers to move in with their families. The Housing Colony is situated in the southwest corner of the gigantic industrial estate.

Many families moved in with the development of the industrial estate, but the only large-scale housing supply for them in Pithampur was the housing colony. However, because from the time of development there was reliance on capital and manpower from Indore city, a large percentage of the staff class who worked in office and administrative positions took company buses from Indore to their workplaces.

The housing colony construction began in 1986 and had a planned area of 22.34 ha (net land area: 20.73 ha, A sector = 9.55 ha, B and C sectors = 11.18 ha). The planned and actual colonies are shown in Figure 11.1, and an overview of land use planning is shown in Table 11.1. For each of A, B and C sectors, housing occupies about half of the planned area. For housing plots in Sector A, as shown in Figure 11.1, MIG flats face the main street, LIG are situated behind these, that, and the EWS houses are located deepest.

For the entire colony, there are 377 MIG units, 808 LIG units and 739 EWS units, but there are large differences in type of housing provided in each sector. Sector A has 46 MIG units, 397 LIG units, and 739 EWS units; of the total 1,182 units, 62.5 per cent are EWS units for lowest income earners. On the other hand, there are 331 MIG units and 411 LIG units in the B and C sectors, but no EWS units. Also, because this colony provides housing for labourers who work in the industrial estate, there are no HIG units.

In 1996 at the time of the survey, 904 units had been completed and sold in A sector and B sectors: 137 MIG, 375 LIG and 392 EWS. There

Table 11.1: The land use plan of Pithampur Housing Colony

Sector	*Land Use*	*ha*	*%*	*Details*	
A	Housing	4.9612 ha	51.93%	MIG (6.5×12 m)	46
				LIG (6.5×9 m)	397
				EWS (4.5×5.5 m)	739
	Open	0.685 ha	7.17%		
	Facilities	0.585 ha	6.12%		
	Circulation	3.3220 ha	34.78%		
B & C	Housing	5.4847 ha	49.03%	MIG (6.5×12 m)	331
				LIG (6.5×9 m)	411
				EWS (4.5×5.5 m)	0
	Open	1.2238 ha	10.94%		
	Facilities	0.962 ha	8.60%	school	0.6260 ha
				social building	0.3360 ha
	Circulation	3.5101 ha	31.41%		
	Reserved for shelterless	0.785 ha			
Total	Housing	10.4459 ha	50.38%	MIG (6.5×12 m)	377
				LIG (6.5×9 m)	808
				EWS (4.5×5.5 m)	739
	Open	1.9088 ha	9.20%		
	Facilities	1.5470 ha	7.46%		
	Circulation	6.8321 ha	32.96%		

Source: Planning Map of Pithampur.

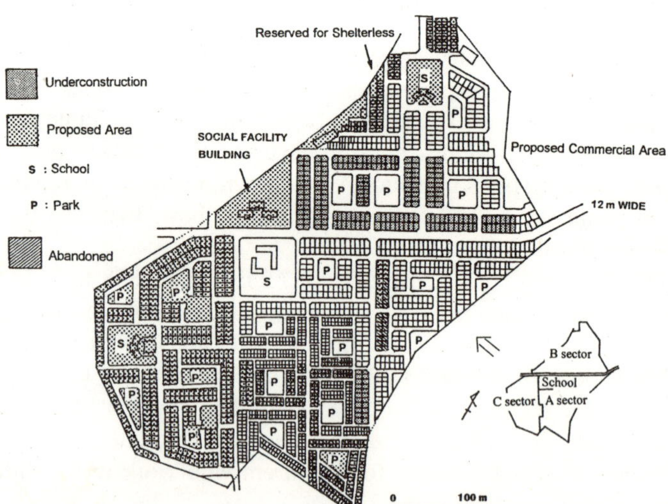

Figure 11.1: The present condition and land use plan in Pithampur Housing Colony

were 60 MIG, 195 LIG, and 113 EWS units under construction with completion targeted for 1997. The planned capacity on completion was 8,000 people, but according to the Housing Board, at the time of the survey there were approximately 5,000 residents.

While new housing is under construction, corporate housing in Sector A for Bajaj Tempo is currently empty and abandoned. Also, empty lots neighbouring the colony are occupied by illegal squatters living in 10 buildings constructed of grass and plastic sheets, and several illegal squatter families are occupying residential buildings under construction in Sector B.

MPAKVN is in charge of residential area zoning and social capital investment infrastructure such as roads for residential areas, while housing construction, supply and management is handled by the MP Housing Board. According to the Housing Board office in this colony, this Bijalpur project is nearly complete, but construction has not yet begun on the second and third schools, shopping centres or community centres, and Sector C is still just barren land. Roads in the colony including the main roads are unpaved, and potholers are constantly filled with household waste water. There are only two grocery stores with a reasonable selection, and in the open spaces in front of residences a few small stores can be found. Residents buy vegetables and other foodstuffs from two-wheeled cart or buy them in the Pithampur town centre which is a short distance away. For clothing, residents sometimes go to shop in the cities of Indore or Mhow.

HOMES IN HOUSING COLONIES AND RESIDENT QUALITIES

Varied State of Housing

Residents were interviewed to reveal the state of housing. Of the approximately 900 completed units, interviews were conducted for 122 units. Of those interviewed there were 16 MIG, 84 LIG and 22 EWS households, and 58.2 per cent of these owned their residences. Looking at the relation between housing type and ownership, 18 of 22 EWS dwellers, 44 of 84 LIG dwellers and 9 of 16 MIG dwellers owned their properties.

All units in this housing colony were built for sale, but there were also a large number of renters because property investments were also allowed. Owners of rental properties were absentee landlords, living in Indore or Mhow. The monthly rent for most MIG renters was over

Rs. 1,000, and two-thirds of LIG renters paid Rs. 500-750 per month.

Most residents who owned their properties learnt of the housing colony from newspapers or government publications. Most renters, on the other hand, heard about the properties from acquaintances. EWS and LIG residents chose their properties solely for employment reasons. On the other hand, in addition to employment reasons, many MIG households cited other reasons such as the quality of units and its convenient location next to the industrial estate.

For appliances and fixtures, as shown in Table 11.2, all units had electric lighting, water, toilets and showers. In terms of durable electric appliances, very few EWS residents had colour televisions, but ownership ratios for LIG and MIG households were high. Colour television ownership was higher in owned homes than rented homes, highlighting the difference in household earning power. Nearly all home buyers across units had gas ranges, but EWS and LIG renters had gas ranges very few. This is partially due to the fact that many renters are single men living alone, but even for households comprising parents and children, less than half of LIG rented homes had gas cooking ranges. The state of the kitchen was an obvious reflection of the household's economic condition. While MIG dwellers had plentiful and varied spices, LIG dwellers had few.

Next, 43.2 per cent LIG dwellers and 77.8 per cent of MIG dwellers owned refrigerators, and ownership rates were higher for homeowners. Similarly, ownership rates of expensive durable goods such as scooters and bicycles were higher for homeowners. Also, higher the MIG income level, higher the ownership rate, highlighting the difference between income levels. Reflecting the high demand for electric appliances in the colony, there were two small-scale electric appliance stores. The penetration of durable goods and daily commodities has picked up speed since the economic liberalisation policies of 1991, and product information learned through television, has shrunken the gap in consumable goods adoption rates between cities and rural areas.

Home owners are making significant home improvement investments such as adding rooms, and painting the inside and outside. For this reason home owners are thought to be more sedentary than renters. However, among the more mobile renters, home maintenance investments such as wall painting are extremely low. Also, as evidenced by their high mobility, the number of possessions they bring with them when moving is low.

As toilets and plumbing, which are still not widely prevalent in

Table 11.2: Ownership of commodities by housing types

	Housing Types											
	EWS				*LIG*				*MIG*			*Total*
	Not own	*Own*	*(NA)*	*Sum*	*Not own*	*Own*	*(NA)*	*Sum*	*Not own*	*Own*	*Sum*	
Radio	8	14	0	22	32	51	1	84	6	10	16	122
TV(mono)	6	16	0	22	26	58	0	84	4	12	16	122
TV(color)	20	2	0	22	68	16	0	84	13	3	16	122
Sewing machine	9	13	0	22	48	36	0	84	9	7	16	122
Gas cooking stove	4	17	1	22	21	63	0	84	2	14	16	122
Kerosene stove	8	13	1	22	39	45	0	84	13	3	16	122
Electric refrigirator	16	5	1	22	58	26	0	84	7	9	16	122
Airconditioner	22	0	0	22	82	2	0	84	16	0	16	122
Bicycle	1	20	1	22	35	48	1	84	7	9	16	122
Motorcycle/Scooter	16	6	0	22	37	47	0	84	7	9	16	122
Car	21	1	0	22	83	1	0	84	13	3	16	122

Source: Field Survey in November 1996.

India, are provided for each home in this colony, and also because of the safe environment and convenient location, many residents were satisfied with their way of living. However, most were dissatisfied with the poor location at the edge of the wide industrial estate, poor road conditions, water supply limitations, water contamination and high cost of living. Even though MPAKVN agreed to provide 3,50,000 litres of water per day, in fact water was only provided for 30 minutes each morning and evening, forcing households to rely on well water and water tanks in the open spaces next to the front entrances. Homemakers even could be seen carrying water from wells dug in public parks. However, because the well water is of extremely poor quality, in terms of water usage, residents are forced into an inconvenient way of living. Even so, compared to Pithampur village which is teeming with workers and traders, this housing colony is hired for its safety.

Residential Households of Middle Class Families

Nuclear family households consisting of parents and children made up 63.1 per cent of all households, but nuclear families with a sibling of the head of the household also reached 13.1 per cent. Joint families living together with parents or grandparents also made up 10.7 per cent of the total. Joint families are common in India's rural regions, but in new localities like this, the living space is too small to support extended family. For compact residences with only one room like those in this housing colony, extended family living is made possible by building additional rooms, and those doing this are 18.9 per cent for head of household in late 20s, 35.3 per cent for those in the early 30s, and 21.3 per cent for those in the late 30s. Younger households account for three-fourths of the total, partly because their children are still little.

There is an elementary school in the colony, but because many middle class parents are concerned about education, a significant number of children can be seen taking buses to attend private elementary schools. Also, not many children in their late teens were seen in the housing colony; this is because junior school and higher educational facilities are not sufficient in Pithampure. To obtain better quality education, most households send their children to large cities like Indore to attend high schools.

Irrespective of owners or renters, most heads of household in EWS and LIG houses was line workers at factories inside the industrial estate. In the LIG houses, in addition to line workers, heads of households had varied occupations such as factory managers or office workers. No MIG home owners were line workers, but there were many self-employed individuals who kept shops or ran businesses. On the other hand, many MIG renters were line workers.

Many EWS and LIG head of households had completed junior education, or become line workers after completing junior school and ITI training. Also the high ratio of LIG and MIG renters with higher educational background reflects their high degree of mobility.

If we look at the occupation structure and closely related caste structure, we find that most home owners and renters, in the LIG and MIG residents are from the upper castes like Brahmin and Rajput. Upper castes are dominant in the EWS residences as well.

In terms of household income, LIG owners and renters earned between Rs. 3,000 and 5,000. More than half of EWS and LIG residents, both renters and owners, made less than Rs. 3,000 per month. The range of income of MIG residents was wide due to the varied occupations, and many renting households had high incomes. From our analysis, we can say that the middle class forms the bulk of this colony.

MOBILITY OF COLONY HOUSEHOLDS

Using habitat movement, we studied the migration characteristics of the residents.

About half–49.2 per cent–were from MP, and most were from nearby districts such as Indore. About 40 per cent were from other states; of these 19.7 per cent were from Maharashtra and 14.8 per cent were from Uttar Pradesh. By habitat type, there were many from Maharashtra in the EWS group, and of these more than half were from Jalgaon, which borders MP.

In terms of previous place of residence, most moved from in-state neighbouring districts such as Indore. They originated from various places inside and outside MP, and the percentage of those who previously lived in neighbouring districts within MP was large. This is the result of movement through large-scale industrial cities such as Indore with many work opportunities.

By educational background, of individuals from both urban and rural areas and from inside and outside of MP, few were highly educated; the majority had completed either elementary education or begun working after completing junior school or attending ITI.

In India, what at first glance appear to be independent city families are actually a branch of extended village families. Many labourers who have lived in cities for even 20-30 years still consider their residential status in these cities as 'temporary'.[5] In other words, those from rural areas maintain strong ties with their places of origin, most (32.5 per cent) visit their home-towns once a year, and 20.5 per cent even go every month or once every two months. In-state labourers from both city and rural areas visit their home-towns especially frequently.

There is large gap in income levels of staff members living in the housing colony and those commuting from Indore. Many of residents in the housing colony have moved from areas outside Indore, and while they have high incomes they are relatively more mobile and do not own their residences.

Most of those commuting from Indore have a history of leaving their home towns and moving from city to city, which contrasts with most housing colony residents for who moved directly to the Pithampur industrial area.

HOUSING COLONIES: THE DREAM AND THE REALITY

As Pithampur Housing Colony, which came up together with the industries, was developed to provide housing for factory workers who moved to the industrial estate, most colony residents are industry-related workers. However, various service industry and construction contractors also live here.

According to Dwyer,[6] housing policies in the Third World generally do not take into account the urbanisation process, especially ignoring issues related to the underlying characteristics of housing issues, and many use mistaken processes. This results in a widespread tendency to serve a privileged few in the middle class, instead of the poor.

In Pithampur Housing Colony which was intended to be a solution for this, even though three types of habitats—MIG, LIG and EWS—are provided assuming different income levels, it has resulted in concentrating middle income residents with specific income levels. On this point Dwyer's argument is supported.

NOTES

1 C. Pugh, *Housing and Urbanisation: A Study of India*, New Delhi: Sage Publication, 1990.
2 A. Bose, *India's Urbanisation 1901-2001,* revd. 2nd edn., New Delhi: Tata McGraw-Hill, 1978.
3 Ibid.

4 R.K. Vishwakarma, *Urban and Regional Planning Policy in India*, New Delhi: Uppal Publishing House, 1981.
5 D.J. Dwyer, *People and Housing in Third World Cities: Perspectives on the Problem of Spontaneous Settlements,* London: Longman, 1975.
6 Ibid.

CHAPTER 12

Urbanisation and Agglomeration of Central Functions

HIROKAZU SAKUNO

URBANISATION OF PITHAMPUR VILLAGE

Pithampur Industrial Growth Centre is made up of three sectors. Sectors 1 and 2 border Pithampur village, which existed before the industrial estate was developed. As of 1971 Pithampur village was 790 ha in size, and of this irrigated arable land was less than 1 per cent (only 9.7 ha), the majority being non-irrigated land. Even though there was plentiful land with agricultural potential, because of insufficient irrigation, agricultural productivity was low. Also 212 ha (26.9 per cent of total area) was used as stock farms or pastures. In this way Pithampur village was a settlement dependent on low productivity agriculture. But industrial estate development would bring remarkable changes.

In Pithampur village today, the old areas with dense private residences (hereafter referred to as the 'old village') are surrounded by which have changed the scenery surrounding the old village. Cultivated land, ranches and pastures are no longer found, to the north of the old village; many stores and offices line the southern edge stretching east and west along State Highway 27 (Mhow-Neemach Road), giving the air of a regular city. This road is at the centre of Pithampur village today, and is it's main road. Several branch roads have been built which connect to this main road, and residential estates are being developed along these roads. Also, the housing colony lines the southeast edge of the Industrial Growth Centre. Even the remnants of the farming village are fast disappearing as houses are being rebuilt as stores and apartments.

The changes in Pithampur village become more evident when considering its population. In 1971 the population of Pithampur village was just 1,066 people. However, this population was compared to surrounding villages, and with a post office, it was one of the lowest order central places. However, the population of 1,286 in 1981 mushroomed approximately tenfold to 11,980 in 1991 with the onset of rapid urbanisation.

A notable characteristic of the population was that it was overwhelmingly male. While the population increased approximately tenfold, the number of households increased about 15 times from 210 to 3,388. These two characteristics can be taken together to surmise that many single men migrated to Pithampur village from other regions. Also, when comparing population by industry between 1971 and 1991, while agricultural workers and labourers only approximately doubled, industrial workers grew from 10 to 4,201 people. This growth is incredible.

The placement of the Industrial Growth Centre next to Pithampur village has resulted in significant and rapid urbanisation. For this reason, in the 1991 census, Pithampur village was no longer classified as a 'village' but as a 'non-municipality.'

Incidentally, before the Industrial Growth Centre was developed, the only public facility at Pithampur was a post office. Today several public facilities as well as government and municipal agencies are now located here. Most of these offices are located in the 'Vikas Building' in the Industrial Growth Centre.

To quote figures, nine government agencies are housed here, including MPAKVN, which the principal developer of the Industrial Growth Centre. With the exception of the post office, all are state or district offices. These agencies are notable in that they have strong onsite management functions, directly overseeing or managing the many factories at the Industrial Growth Centre. Also, agencies other than MPAKVN are new organisations, established here in the 1990s.

Most public agencies are located in the Industrial Growth Centre not only due to the infrastructure here, but also because they are developing the social infrastructure necessary for companies and workers, and agencies maintaining and managing roads, water supply, electricity and sewer system are located here. *Gram Panchayat* and the Pithampur Sub Police Station located inside the old village are the only other government agencies.

Additionally, public facilities such as hospitals and schools are also located there. A public library and high school are located next to the PWD Rest House to the west of the Pithampur village centre, and these facilities were planned as part of the Industrial Growth Centre development project. There is also an elementary school and boys' and girls' junior high schools in the village centre, but these basic educational functions are present in almost any village. Other than these schools, there is one public elementary school in the housing colony. However, according to the interviewees, there are 18 private elementary schools and 2 private junior high schools in the village. Especially notable is the number of private elementary schools is overwhelmingly greater than the number of public elementary schools.

While public facilities such as hospitals and high schools were built as part of the planned Industrial Growth Centre project, due to rapid population growth following urbanisation, the demand is greater than originally planned. As a result, the Industrial Growth Centre appears to be causing bipolar development, as evidenced in the proliferation of private elementary schools, the disorganised growth of educational facilities and the planned and unplanned regional changes.

CONCENTRATION OF CORE FUNCTIONS IN PITHAMPUR VILLAGE

As previously noted, shops and offices in Pithampur village line the main road for approximately 3 km. A significant number of shops are also concentrated in the old village and alongside roads south of the main road. However, from their numbers, overwhelmingly most shops line the main road. Therefore, for this research, shopkeepers along this road were interviewed. Also, for shops in which interviews could not be performed, judging by the external appearance or through interviews with neigh houring shopkeepers, we learned the type of business and position of all shops and offices that faced this main road. Most shops were retail, eating and drinking, and service related businesses, but there were also some public service facilities such as health clinics and banks. However, because their external appearance were largely the same, in this chapter we refer to them as a whole as shops.

It is interesting to note that most of these shops had the same general layout. The shop fronts were approximately 4 m wide and 6-8 m in depth. The side facing the road for all shops was open with no doors, and at closing time a shutter would be closed. Hardly any of these shops were standalone buildings, but were in groups of 3-10 inside one or two storey cement structures. In buildings with two levels, the second storey was used for various purposes such as living area, rented apartment, or the office of another business.

We divided these shops into eight categories. Parallel to Japan's industry categorisation, we categorised the shops into 'Clothes, belongings etc.', 'Food', 'Bicycle, fittings, general merchandise', 'Others', 'Eating and drinking' and 'Services'. Also, for repair and manufacturing of bicycles and machines, which can be thought to be included in the 'Services' category, we made a category 'Manufacturing and repair.' Businesses with a public aspect, such as banks and health clinics, were separately categorised as 'Finance and medical' (see Table 12.1).

We found that a total of 276 shops lined the main road. By business type, an overwhelming number were 'Service' businesses, with 77 shops (27.9 per cent of the total), or close to one-third. Next, there were 52 'Bicycle, fittings, general merchandise' shops (18.8 per cent), 39 'Food' shops (14.1 per cent), 32 'Manufacturing and repair' shops (11.6 per cent), and 29 'Clothes, belongings, etc.' shops (10.5 per cent). Overall, there were more 'Bicycle, fittings, general merchandise' and 'Manufacturing and repair' shops than shops providing daily goods, allowing us to surmise that the types of shops in this commercial agglomeration were different from typical commercial agglomerations.

To closely examine this, let us further subcategorise the types of goods sold and services provided. An overwhelming number of shops were Transportaticn offices. Next, there were 20 'Telephone Booth (STD)' shops (7.2 per cent), 19 'Utensil' shops (6.9 per cent), 18 'Bicycle, motorised cycle repair' shops (6.5 per cent), 17 'General food stores' (6.2 per cent), 16 'Electronic Itɔms' shops and 'Restaurants' (each 5.8 per cent), and 15 'Building Material' shops (5.4 per cent). There were many shops that specialised in daily goods or services such as 'Utensil', 'General Foods Store', and 'Restaurant', but there was also a relatively large number of shops selling or repairing non-daily items such as 'Transportation Office', 'Building Materials' and 'Bicycle, Motorised Cycle Repair'. The latter of these are thought to be office service businesses dependent on demand from factories in the area.

Also, according to the data on the year of opening of shops, only six shops had opened before 1985, the year that basic development began on the Pithampur Industrial Growth Centre. Of course, many shops from that time may have closed or relocated, we can safely assume that there were not as many shops along the main road at that time. Until the early 1990s, each year brought more shops. However, growth of shops was more prolific after 1994; 36 shops (24.8 per cent) opened in 1996, the year of the survey.

Next, in leins of management, of 145 shops, the overwhelming majority—133—were one man operations. Many shops were 'managed

Table 12.1: Classification and numbers of shops in Pithampur (1996)

Classification	*Mark*	*Type of shops*	*Total*		*Interview survey*	
			no.	*%*	*no.*	*%*
Clothes, belongings etc.	CL	Cloth	6	2.2	3	2.1
	RC	Readymade clothes	10	3.6	10	6.9
	TA	Tailoring	7	2.5	3	2.1
	OR	Ornaments	2	0.7	2	1.4
	SH	Shoes	4	1.4	3	2.1
Subtota			29	10.5	21	14.5
Food	GF	General food store (grocery)	17	6.2	12	8.3
	DR	Drink	2	0.7	2	1.4
	VE	Vegetable	3	1.1	2	1.4
	SW	Sweet	8	2.9	4	2.8
	GR	Grain	1	0.4	0	0.0
	EG	Egg	4	1.4	4	2.8
	TO	Tobacco	2	0.7	1	0.7
	OT	Others	2	0.7	0	0.0
Subtotal			39	14.1	25	17.2
Bicycle, fittings, general merchandise	BB	Bicycle and motorbicycle	2	0.7	1	0.7
	BM	Building material	15	5.4	6	4.1
	UT	Utensil	19	6.9	12	8.3
	EL	Electronic items	16	5.8	10	6.9
Subtotal			52	18.8	29	20
Others	ME	Medicine	3	1.1	2	1.4
	AC	Agricultural chemicals	2	0.7	1	0.7
	FU	Fuel	3	1.1	1	0.7
	BS	Books and stationery	2	0.7	2	1.4
	MS	Music shop	4	1.4	3	2.1
	WA	Watch	3	1.1	1	0.7
Subtotal			17	6.2	10	6.9
Eating and drinking	RE	Restaurant	16	5.8	7	4.8
	TC	Tea and coffee shop	3	1.1	3	2.1
Subtotal			19	6.9	10	6.9
Service	BR	Barber	10	3.6	5	3.4
	LA	Laundry	2	0.7	2	1.4
	PS	Photo studio	1	0.4	0	0.0
	TB	Telephone booth	20	7.2	9	6.2
	RO	Real estate office	1	0.4	1	0.7
	CO	Copy	4	1.4	2	1.4
	HO	Hotel	3	1.1	2	1.4
	TR	Transportation office	33	12.0	7	4.8
	OF	Other offices	3	1.1	1	0.7
Subtotal			77	27.9	29	20.0
Manufacturing and repair	MR	Machine repairing	8	2.9	7	4.8
	BR	Bicycle, motorbicycle repairing	18	6.5	7	4.8
	FM	Flour mill	6	2.2	3	2.1
Subtotal			32	11.6	17	11.7
Finance and medical	BA	Bank	3	1.1	0	0.0
	CC	Clinic	8	2.9	4	2.8
Subtotal			11	4.0	4	2.8
Grand Total			276	100.0	145	100.0

Source: Field survey in November 1996.

together with family or friends', but only a handful were 'company run', The results clearly show that retail and service businesses are generally single-store, one-man operations. However, one notable characteristic is that a few businesses such as the transportation shops dominant in Pithampur village were run as larger company operations.

WORKERS ENGAGED IN CENTRAL FUNCTIONS IN PITHAMPUR VILLAGE

Most shopkeepers lived in Pithampur village, neighbouring districts such as Dhar, Mhow and Indore.

Let us look at the social attributes of these shopkeepers from the perspective of religion and caste (see Table 12.2). Of valid responses received from 123 shopkeepers, 100–the overwhelming majority (or 81.3 per cent) were Hindu, 15 (12.2 per cent) were Muslims, and the remainder were a handful of Jains, Christians and Sikhs. Of these, for Hindu jati, upper castes such as Brahmin and Rajput were 48.0 per cent (of the 100 Hindus), making up an overwhelming majority. Of the remainder, 14 (14.0 per cent) of shopkeepers belonged to Other Backward Castes, and only 6 (6.0 per cent) belonged to a lower caste. Also, only 3 shop owners belonged to Scheduled Castes (3.0 per cent), and there were no Scheduled Tribe shop owners.

The majority of shop owners (92 or 84.4 per cent), were Hindus; 14 (12.8 per cent) were Muslims; 2 (1.8 per cent) were Christian; 1 (0.9 per cent) was Jain. Caste composition of shop owners was almost same as for shopkeepers.

First, while there were many shopkeepers from the upper castes, there were more shop owners from Other Backward Castes such as the Lodhi and Nai. Since members of these castes had lived in Pithampur village from before its industrialisation, it is thought that original Pithampur residents opened shops along the main road. Some shop owners also ran their own shops, but there are also cases where the building owner rented the shop out. Also, there was no Scheduled Tribe or Scheduled Caste shop owners.

Incidentally, the years the shopkeepers began their current trade differed largely. As expected, while more shops opened in recent years, there was a wide spread. We can see that shopkeepers who began operations in the 1980s are especially numerous. Taken together with the fact that in recent years shops were rapidly being opened in Pithampur village, it appears that most shopkeepers had shops in other regions and came to Pithampur village expecting growth.

Table 12.2: Caste of shopkeepers and shopowners in Pithampur (1996)

Religion	*Rank of Hindu Caste*	*Name of Hindu Jati*	*Shopkeepers' No.*	*Shop owners' No.*
Hindu	Upper Caste	Agarwal	3	1
		Brahmin	14	6
		Gujjar/Gujar	2	2
		Kayastha	0	2
		Maratha	2	0
		Patel/Patidar	13	8
		Rajput	14	6
		Subtotal	48	25
	Lower Caste	Baniya/Mahajan	3	7
		Kumhar	3	2
		Subtotal	6	9
	Other Backward Caste	Kulmis	2	0
		Lodhi/Pathria	6	21
		Nai/Barber	6	9
		Thakur	0	2
		Subtotal	14	32
	Scheduled Caste	Chamar	1	0
		Dhobi	2	0
		Subtotal	3	0
	Unknown Caste	Maheshwari/Bauiys	4	0
		Meena	2	2
		Momedian	5	7
		Raghuvanshi	3	2
		Rathone	2	2
		Subtotal	16	13
	Caste N.A.		13	13
		Total	100	92
Sikh			1	0
Jain			3	1
Muslim			15	14
Christian			2	2
N.A.			2	0
	Grand Total		123	109

Source: Field survey in November 1996.

Finally, professionally 44 (33.3 per cent) shopkeepers were previouly students. It is notable that new graduates were prove to opening shops. Next, 33 shopkeepers (22.8 per cent) had worked in the primary industry; 31 (21.4 per cent) were in the tertiary industry; and 17 (11.7 per cent) had worked in the secondary industry. In contrast, only 6 (4.1 per cent) had tended shops after working in agriculture, leading to the conclusion that not many Pithampur village residents made the leap from agriculture to shopkeeping.

From the above, we can see that workers supporting the central functions of Pithampur village came from other regions; few came from careers in agriculture, and that the most common pattern was those in tertiary commerce saw growth potential in Pithampur village and came here to open shops. Likewise, it is notable that new graduates opened shops.

PLANNED REGIONAL URBANISATION AND AGGLOMERATION OF CENTRAL FUNCTIONS

We earlier discussed the rapid regional changes seen in Pithampur, village, caused by the location of Pithampur Industrial Growth Centre. Pithampur village today has three simultaneous functions: a housing function for mainly factory labourers, a central function which spontaneously arose to serve an increased population, a central function of providing goods or services to surrounding factories.

Industrial Growth Centre development in Pithampul and elswhere provides not just factory plots for locating industry, but also infrastructure improvements linked to industrial production such as roads, water, electricity and sewage systems. It also provides lifestyle related infrastructure such as medical, communications, education, and police facilities. Together with the effects of the natural urbanisation caused by industrial labourers taking up residence as previously discussed, the growth of Pithampur village was greatly effected by policy-driven infrastructure and housing developments by agencies responsible for Industrial Growth Centre development. These two aspects are seen also in agglomeration of central functions. For instance, while we see proliferation of private hospitals and schools, public high schools and hospitals are also planned and developed.

In this way, Industrial Growth Centre development under government guidance has resulted in efforts to provide infrastructure and residential facilities through policies, and to build a liveable city close to work and home. However, this development has led to an avalanche of labourers looking for work, and signs of spontaneous agglomeration of central functions can be seen, in the rapid proliferation of shops targeting this large-scale market. In this way, we can see that there is a two-sided characteristic of planned development and natural growth in the areas surrounding the Industrial Growth Centre.

CHAPTER 13

Transformation of Rural Community Neighbouring the Industrial Estate: Case Study of Village C

MUNENORI SAWA AND HITOSHI ARAKI

ISSUES OF RURAL COMMUNITIES IN BACKWARD REGIONS OF INDIA

Various issues such as population, poverty, education, women and caste have been regularly cited as problems for India's rural communities. According to the census data of 2001, India's population is 1.027 billion people. Overall population growth was 21 per cent between 1991 and 2001; this growth shows no signs of letting up. This high population growth is one of the obstacles to resolving India's poverty.

Poverty is most serious in rural regions where approximately 72 per cent of the overall population lives in poverty. Almost 50 per cent of the rural population lives in conditions of absolute poverty, unable to obtain the minimum amount of calories required for sustenance. Additionally, there are great differences in the literacy rate: 79 per cent can read in urban areas while only 49 per cent can read in rural areas, 76 per cent men can read against only 54 per cent women. These problems are interrelated, but at the root of them is the poverty of rural residents. India's unique caste system further complicates these problems. However, the state of affairs greatly differs by region, and in backward regions, conditions are thought to be especially critical.

In this chapter, by focusing on a backward region, we take one rural village which was directly affected by economic liberalisation, as a case study to find out how change manifests in India's rural communities, and whether or not these problems were resolved. Specifically, we reveal the impact and the influx of industrialisation on employment and agriculture, new residents and social structure of rural villages.

CASE STUDY—AN OVERVIEW OF VILLAGE C

Village C is about 3 km from Pithampur Industrial Growth Centre. With the coming of industries, it is currently facing an influx of new industrial labourer residents. Also, with increased production of vegetables and dairy products to meet industrial estate residents, agricultural management is also changing.

The age composition of original residents was a typical pyramid characteristic of populations with many births and many deaths and commonly seen in rural villages in developing nations (see Figure 13.1). Particularly notable is the high birth rate and high infant death rate.

There are glaring gender and caste differences. For instance, upper castes own more farmland, and upper caste males have better educational qualifications. Village C has a multi-caste social structure and the indigenous residents belong to eight castes: the uppermost Brahmin caste, the Khati, Panchal and Nai, which are members of Other Backward Castes, the Chamar, Bagri and Balai, which are the Scheduled Castes, and the Bhil which is a Scheduled Tribe.

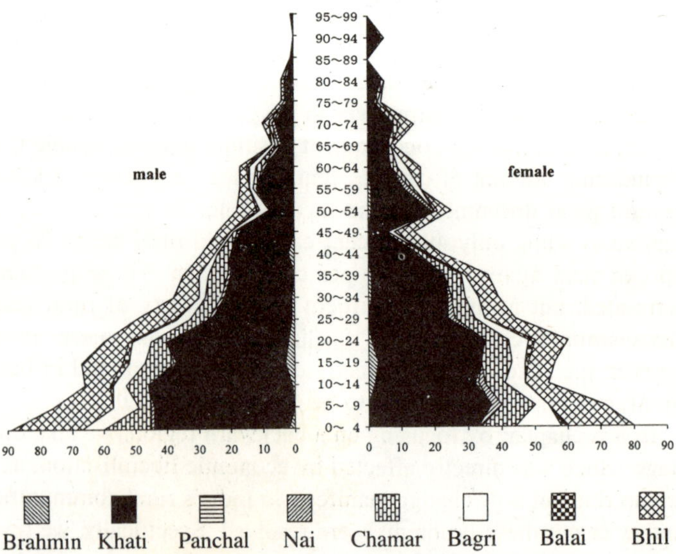

Source: Field survey in 1996.

Figure 13.1: Age distribution of locals in Village C in 1996 (caste-wise)

GROWTH OF NON-AGRICULTURAL EMPLOYMENT

Due to many new factories being established following the development of Pithampur Industrial Growth Centre, the varied and rich employment opportunities were created. In addition to the demand for factory workers, there was need for labourers in factory-related construction and shipping, as well as employment in service firms, restaurants and shops. This growth of the regional labour market had a large impact on nearby rural villages, causing differentiation in the occupations of residents.

As discussed in Chapter 10, the industrial labour market in Pithampur comprised the four levels of executive, staff, permanent worker and temporary worker, and there were large differences in the education levels of these four groups.

The original residents of Village C belonged to the two bottom groups, permanent worker and temporary worker, and were little impacted by the labour market for executives and staff. Furthermore, the castes from which employees were hired were limited. Factories only hired as permanent workers men who had received at least lower secondary education and these were usually members of the Brahmin or the dominant Khati caste, or members of the Chamar caste, who took advantage of scholarship programmes and reservation systems afforded to members of Scheduled Castes (see Figure 13.2).

Some males with elementary or lower secondary education from Khati, Chamar and Bagri castes, and the Bhil Scheduled Tribe were included in the lowest temporary worker group of the industrial labour market. However, illiterates with no education who were excluded from this industrial labour market had no alternative but to remain in the low paying agricultural labour market. It was virtually impossible for them to move to the higher paying industrial labour market in the future. The younger members of these families also had to tend to household chores such as tending livestock or carrying water, so they did not all complete compulsory education. These people were thus effectively shut out from higher paying work opportunities.

Some from the Khati agricultural castes met success in commercial agriculture, producing vegetables and soybeans for large-scale managed farms. Some Khati and Bagri families successfully responded to increased demand for milk and specialised in livestock management of mainly dairy cows. Some were successful in obtaining higher paying jobs as contractors who procure construction workers, temporary factory workers and workers performing odd job. Only men were able to be

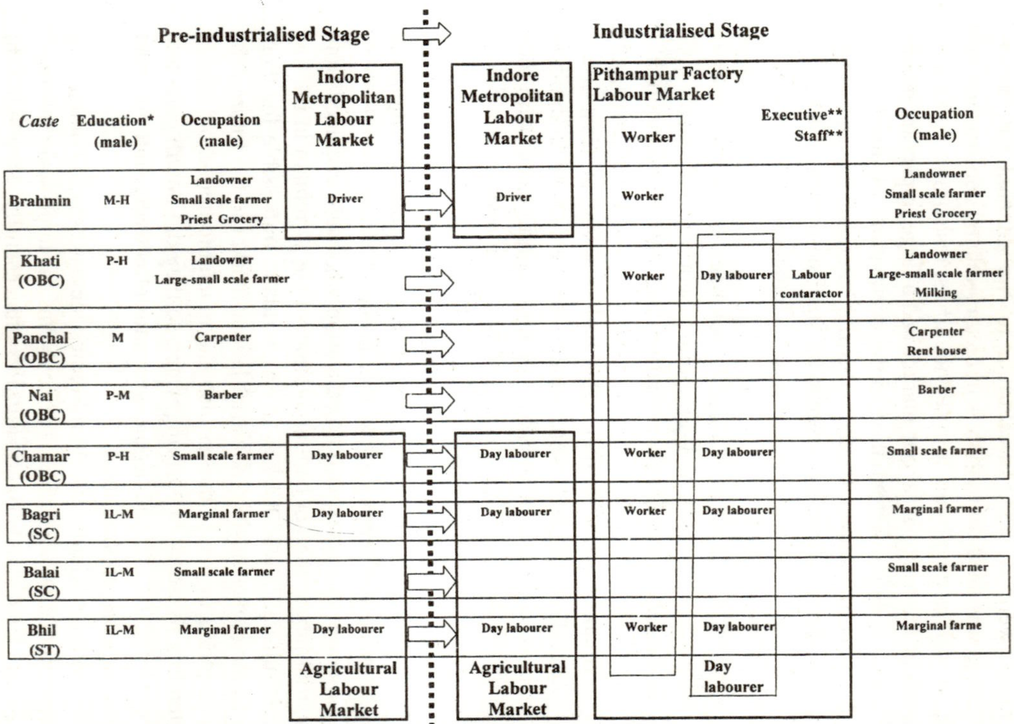

Notes: * IL: Illiterate P: Primary level M: Middle level H: Higher level
** Executive and Staff: villager can not be involed.

Figure 13.2: Reorganisation of labour market and social stratification in Village C

employed as industrial workers; employment of women was still extremely limited.

CHANGES IN AGRICULTURAL STRUCTURE

Agriculture Moving Toward Commercialisation

The main cash crop of Village C today is soybeans. India is a growing soybean export nation and Madhya Pradesh is India's largest soybean producing region. Soybean producers are concentrated in Indore and its surrounding; Village C sits in a corner of one of India's largest soybean producing regions.

Indore's demand for food products is also great. There are four wholesale markets in the city, together serving as a major distribution centre for this region's agricultural products. Excluding produce kept for its own demand, most of Village C's crops are sent to these markets.

Of the total 215 households in the village, 135 own farmland, and 80 do not. This figure includes newcomers who arrived for employment at Pithampur (see Table 13.1). Excepting original residents engaged in traditional services such as haircutting, most work in agriculture.

In the biggest farmhouses (10 *bigha* or about 2.5 ha), or more farmland, modernisation through usage of tractors or chemical fertilisers is evident. On the other hand, smaller farms adopt fewer of these modern techniques. This shows the different economic conditions of these farmhouses.

Table 13.1: Number of farm households by size of agricultural land (owned)

Size (Bigha)	*Number of households*	(%)
Over 50	1	0.5
Over 40	2	0.9
Over 30	1	0.5
Over 20	7	3.3
Over 10	25	11.6
Over 5	40	18.6
Under 5	59	27.4
Landless	80	37.2
Total	215	100.0

Source: Field survey in 1996.

Soybean and wheat are representative crops, but soybean is predominantly grown as a *Kharif* crop and wheat as a *Rabi* crop. Also, most soybean farming was begun 10-20 years ago. Before that time, self-sustaining crops like corn and sorghum were grown. While all the soybean crop is grown for sale, wheat is still primarily grown for self-consumption.

Other than these, potato, garbanzo bean, and garlic are grown as *Rabi* crops, corn is a *Kharif* season crop, and sugarcane and cauliflower are grown in both seasons. Cauliflower, garlic and potato are especially sold as cash crops. This trend is very common in large farms, but small-scale farms generally do not grow them. Some linkage with markets outsider MP was also found, especially for cauliflower and potatoes. Additionally, there were many dairy farms; at the time of the survey 105 farms were producing for both self consumption and for sale, and two milk buyers regularly came to buy the products.

Changes in Agriculture due to Industrial Estate Development

Housing developments continue in Pithampur and with the population growth the demand for food products is also growing. Capitalising on this opportunity, changes can be seen in the agriculture in the neighbouring areas. Changes seen in Village C were the periodic market in Pithampur and shipment of milk.

Pithampur's periodic market met the demands of new residents, at the time of the survey the market was held on Saturdays. Buying and selling was done in street stalls.

Most shipments of soybean, wheat and some vegetable products went to markets in Indore, but since the development of the industrial estate, the number of farmers taking their produce to the period market have increased. Sales in this market are done by the grower himself and this is thought to be one of the strengths this market delivery method. Another attraction may be the absence of transportation costs.

On the other hand, many survey respondents said that the large-scale farms still sent most of their produce to Indore and do not participate in the Pithampur market. This is because these large farms can deliver more products to Indore markets than the period market in Pithampur, and can more efficiently sell their produce in large city markets than at small periodic markets.

Of the people interviewed, about half take their produce to Indore's markets, while the others half take their product to Pithampur's Saturday market. However, as already seen, overall there is a tendency for large farms to go to Indore and small farms to go to Pithampur. In terms of volume, vegetables going to Pithampur totalled about one-third of those going to Indore.

We can see here the different market strategies of different farms. In other words, large-scale farms with high product volume prefer the markets at Indore which are geared for big trade sizes. Because they may not be able to sell all of their products at Pithampur in small trades, large farms see large shipments as effective in reducing transportation costs. Small farms, on the other hand, have low shipping costs and low distribution level margins, and are drawn to Pithampur's market where their crops can be quickly converted into cash. To this extent, Pithampur's development has helped to bring a market and provide cash to small-scale farms in surrounding villages.

For instance, Farm A is a large farm with 13 *bigha* (about 3.3 ha) of farmland. The owners say they send all their vegetable crops such as cauliflower, potato, eggplant and garlic, as well as wheat, soybean and garbanzo bean crops to the produce market in Indore. Large-scale Farm B also occasionally takes its produce to Pithampur, but seventh in size with 8 *bigha* (about 2 ha), the farm owners say their trips to the Saturday market by bicycle have increased since the industrial development, but only 10 per cent of their total product volume can be sold here, and their main destination remains the city markets.

Relatively small Farm C, however, sends about half its produce to the markets in Indore and about half to Pithampur's periodic market. Farm D, which owns 5 *bigha* (about 1.3 ha) of farmland, previously sent its cauliflower and eggplant to Indore, but now sends all its produce to the periodic market.

Pithampur's milk demand has also impacted Village C's agriculture. There are currently two known milk collecting businesses, but in the early 1980s, residents from neighbouring villages would use a light commercial vehicle to collect milk from their village and neighbouring villages, and sell in Indore. However, after the industrial development in Pithampur, the milk has been sent to and consumed in Pithampur which is closer. Then in about the mid-1990s, one village resident began a milk collection business. Each milk collector attaches special milk cans to motorbikes or bicycles and collects between 60-90 litres per vehicle. One collector sends the milk to company cafeterias run by his family in Pithampur, and the other sends to shops in Pithampur, and together with milk collected from other villages, it is then delivered to individual customers in Pithampur, like tea shops and cafeterias.

INFLUX OF NEWCOMERS

The industrial estate is continuing to absorb new workers and newcomers continue to flow into nearby rural villages. In what way did they come to live in this case study village?

Most newcomers are 20-24 years-old men, and their wives and children (see Figure 13.3). There are more males than females. Also, it is notable that their educational level is significantly higher than the original village population.

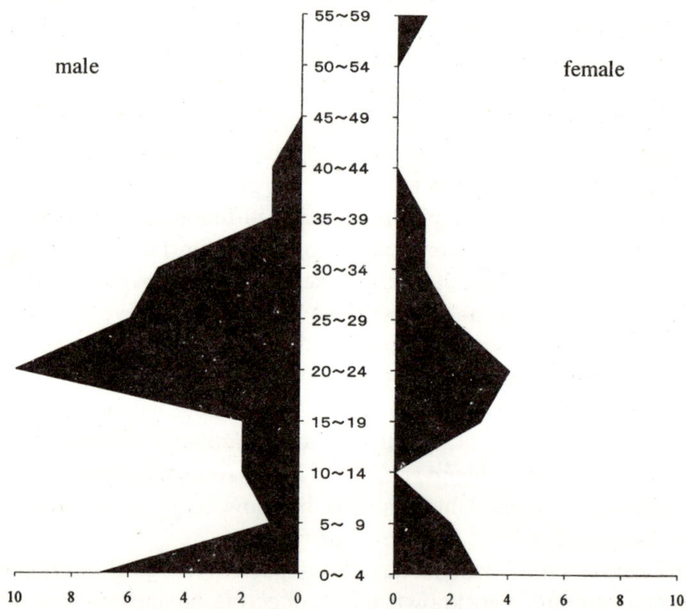

Source: Field survey in 1996.

Figure 13.3: Age profile of newcomers in Village C in 1996

Let us look at the background of the newcomers. Men from rural villages, after leaving school, first move to Pithampur Industrial Estate as labourers seeking work. Those with good education are employed as permanent workers, and the others are employed as temporary workers. Then, some of these workers seeking low rental housing move to the neighbouring Village C. However, because temporary workers and day labourers have limited employment periods, they may move in and out of the industrial estate in search of work, and if unable to find employment many return to their home-towns. Most newcomers to Village C invite their wives and children to stay with them, but those who still have unstable low incomes leave their family behind in their home-towns. What has made this sort of single migration possible is the joint family system, in which siblings live together with their parents even after marriage, and work on the farm, share finances, and participate in festivals.

Living periods of newcomers at rented residences is short–between two and three years. After they secure full-time work and a stable income, they move to more comfortable and more expensive rented residences at Pithampur. However, if they feel it will be unlikely for them to find this kind of stable work, they return to their home regions.

Newcomers searching for rental properties almost entirely rely on information obtained from friends or relatives. Landlords do not make special efforts to advertise their properties and there are no media that provide real estate information. This is one factor responsible for chain migrations, where relatives or migrants from the same caste and hometown tend to live near each other in the destination.

In determining whether to settle in a certain property, Village C is positively regarded for its low rent and good living conditions (air/drinking water). Also, newcomers place emphasis on the caste make-up of other renters in the property they are considering. Especially, vegetarians from upper castes are strict about non-vegetarians or renters from Scheduled Castes or Scheduled Tribes.

IMPACT ON VILLAGE SOCIAL STRUCTURE

What impact has the industrialisation of Pithampur had on the social make-up of neighbouring rural villages? We consider this from the perspective of inter-caste relations.

Before being impacted by industrialisation, Village C was dominated by the landowning Khati caste, the dominant caste in this village. The Bagris and Bhils worked as day workers in the farms owned by Khatis, and farm equipment was maintained by the Panchals. Brahmins provided the priests for the village's Hindu temple, and Nais provided barber services for village residents. In this way, a self-sustaining division of labour had developed in the village around farming, typical of traditional Indian farming communities (see Figure 13.4).

Under these conditions, for small-time farmers or those without land (especially Bagri and Bhil), day-to-day employment at Khati-owned

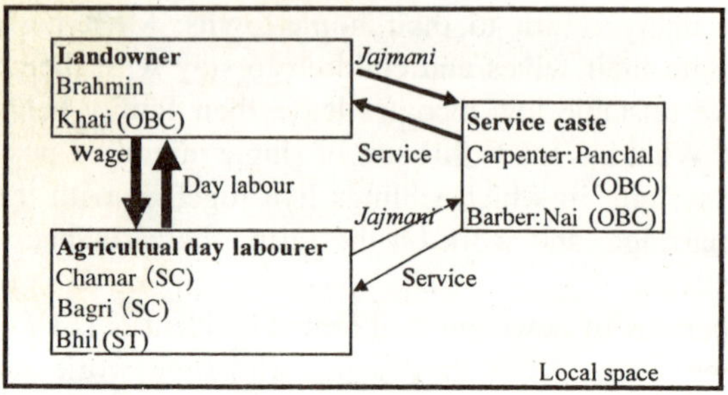

Figure 13.4: The complementary division of labour in Village C before industrialisation

farms was an unavoidable necessity to survive. The *panchayat*, the village level government, was also structured to favour the dominant Khati caste. For instance, in the *panchayat* (village C and two neighbouring villages formed a *panchayat*,) election held in 1988, one Khati and one Brahmin were elected as representatives for village C. Those with a say in political matters such as distribution of government aid were limited to those from upper castes. What impact has industrial growth had on the village's political structure? In the 1994 election, the *panchayat* only contained Village C. The village was divided into 10 electoral wards and one *panchayat* representative was selected from each of these.

As Village C was clearly divided along caste lines, there was a clear relation between each electoral ward and caste. For this reason, except for the Panchal, Nai and Balai with very low populations, one member of each caste making up the original village population was elected as *panchayat* representative. However, the leader of the village *panchayat*, the *Sarpanch*, was chosen from the dominant Kahti caste. Of the *Sarpanch* (1 person) and 10 village *panchayat* representatives, government regulations dictated that at least 5 must be women. However, these female representatives were merely cosmetic in their presence—their husbands held the actual power. These changes in the electoral system are intended to protect the Scheduled Castes and Scheduled Tribes, and women who will have low social standing in India. However, in reality, the daily wages for agricultural labourers employed on a day-to-day remain lower than the legal minimum, and lower castes harbour great frustration toward the upper castes. But fearing retributions and loss of employment, the Scheduled Caste Bagri and Scheduled Tribe Bhil, daily wage agricultural workers, do not complain against the Khati landowners. Also, even though the electoral system was reformed to benefit lower castes and women, women *panchayat* representatives in reality handed the power to their husbands, and status quo is maintained.

In this way, even while the village economy is being subjected to changes of industrialisation, the landowning Khati caste remains the dominant caste and controls Village C. Meanwhile, the Bagri and Bhil remain subservient to the Khati as agricultural labourers on Khati farms. One possible factor for this is that Pithampur's industrial labour market growth has only absorbed men with at least elementary or secondary education and the rest remain in the agricultural labour market, where they remain subservient to the Khati landowners. Also, Pithampur's day labourers and odd-job labourers, unlike permanent factory workers or temporary workers with direct contracts with the factory, are dependent on the work given to them, and thus cannot escape from subjugation. In this way, even though *jajmani* system has disappeared, the essential village local political structure remains unchanged.

Education plays a strong role in the class hierarchy in the labour market and in the caste system in Hindu society. But caste system is not necessarily a predictor of the educational qualification and economic standards. For instance, there are some Scheduled Caste members have succeeded in achieving permanent employment due to better education through scholarship programmes or reservation systems, taking advantage of the industrialisation to improve their economic standing.

For this reason, better education has been repeatedly cited as a necessity to resolve the problems of poverty and subservience in lower castes. Certainly, while scholarship programmes and reservation systems for lower castes have had some degree of success, in reality many rural residents remain so poor that they are unable to take advantage of these systems.

The Integrated Rural Development Programme (IRDP) aims to improve the economic standing of the poor by providing the materials and training skills. However, the reality is that village landowner leaders have used their political clout to effectively use these programmes to their own advantage. For this reason, it is important and necessary to use IRDP for the intended purpose of helping the poor in rural villages to be able to ease their living, for instance by buying their own dairy cattle. Also, these programmes should improve literacy. However, at the root there is a need for reforms to distribute the ownership of farmland, which is concentrated in the upper castes.

PART IV

INDUSTRIAL ESTATE DEVELOPMENT AND INDUSTRIALISATION IN A METROPOLITAN AREA

CHAPTER 14

Growth of the National Capital Region and Development of NOIDA

HIDENORI OKAHASHI

GROWTH OF THE DELHI METROPOLITAN AREA AND THE NATIONAL CAPITAL REGION

The Delhi Metropolitan Area (DMA) underwent rapid industrial growth after the 1970s, and since the advent of economic liberalisation, it has become a major centre of industrialisation in India. This region's industrialisation is especially significant because it spurred industrial growth in India's inland areas that had been industrially weak until this time. It also impacted the Hindi Belt states in the northern regions, which face acute poverty.

With the objective of relieving overcrowding and continuing sustainable growth, a planned region called National Capital Region (NCR) has been established in the DMA. Centred around the Union Territory and now state of Delhi, the region also includes portions of the three neighbouring states Uttar Pradesh (UP), Haryana, and Rajasthan. In looking at the expansion and growth of the DMA, it is most effective to consider it from this scale.

In this chapter, after considering Delhi and the surrounding industry from a national scale, we look at NCR which has served as the site of industrial estate development. Furthermore, we consider the state of these industrial estates through case studies of UP state's NOIDA and Greater NOIDA, the largest 'Integrated Industrial Parks' (IIPs) in NCR.

INDUSTRIALISATION OF NCR AND INDUSTRIAL ESTATE DEVELOPMENT

The Rise of Delhi Industrial Area

After the 1970s, in terms of capital investment, eastern India stagnated, the west and the south grew, but notably, a new trend of growth of NCR around Delhi emerged. This industrial investment trend can also be seen after the 1991 shift to an open economic system.

The industrial investment in Maharashtra and Gujarat–17 and 14 per cent respectively–exceeds the 10 per cent all India average, clearly showing the western advantage. On the other hand, the number is less than 1 per cent for eastern states such as Bihar, Orissa, and West Bengal–progress of stagnation. The northern and southern states occupy an intermediate position between these extremes, especially the states around Delhi–UP, Haryana, Rajasthan.

Industrialisation in Delhi, the central city of the NCR, advanced rapidly after independence. Refugees trooping in after the separation of India and Pakistan brought with them technical and business expertise, and the number of factories and labourers sharply increased. Factory decentralisation was suggested early on as a way to handle industrial growth in Delhi.

The suggestion was implemented in the 1957 Delhi Development Act and the 1962 Delhi Master Plan. While factory decentralisation was being enforced in regions near Delhi, industrial estate development was continuing simultaneously under DDA leading to an increase in industrial agglomeration. After the 1970s, together with strengthened government policies to promote industrial decentralisation, industries were even more pressured to move to areas in the NCR surrounding Delhi.

The following six points are thought to be important factors in the recent industrial growth in the NCR.

1. There is a large consumer market with a large middle class in Delhi, and this location is advantageous to enter the growing domestic market by first targeting the northern India market.
2. This is especially true for foreign capital arriving after economic liberalisation. By locating industry in Delhi, various external economies are enjoyed, such as ease of doing business with government and other corporations.
3. A well trained workforce can be easily secured.
4. Large scale industrial estates have been developed in NOIDA and Greater NOIDA, and the prospects of obtaining space in one of these estates are good.
5. Information gathering and networking opportunities are better, improving the possibilities for technological innovation.

6. Overseas contacts can be easily made for foreign capital firms, and the living conditions in a big city are favourable for expatriates. Based on the above points, the growth potential is expected to remain strong in the future.

Industrial Estate Development in the NCR

The NCR is divided into (1) Delhi state (1,483 sq km) at the centre, (2) DMA, a region combined with Delhi state (1,696 sq km), and (3) other regions (27,063 sq km). Because region (2) is close to Delhi state, it has attracted the maximum industry and population. The most central cities here are Ghaziabad, NOIDA, Faridabad, and Gurgaon (see Figure 14.1). (3) is an extremely large region with a rural feel, and to serve the objective of a more balanced NCR growth, seven Priority Towns have been established as growth centres.

When considering the industrial estate development area for each city in relation to this NCR growth plan, the significance of these growth

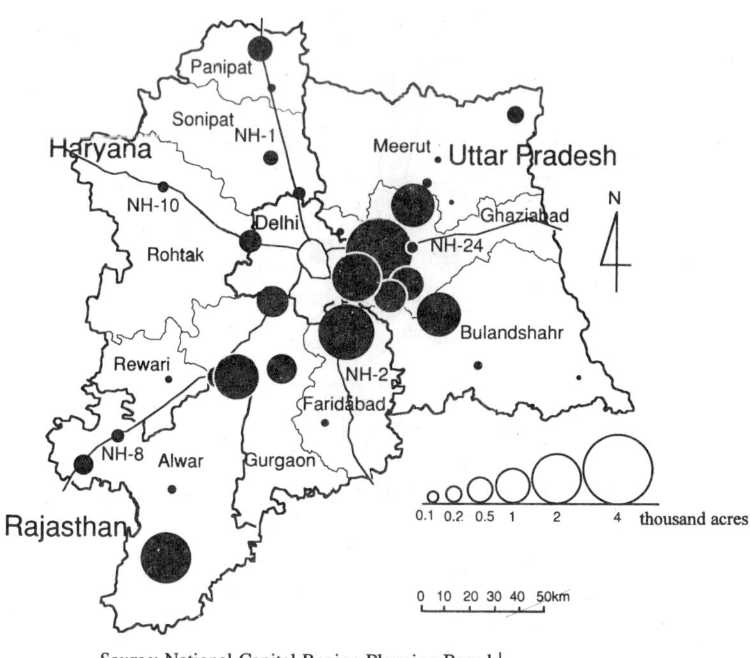

Source: National Capital Region Planning Board.[1]

Figure 14.1: Growth centres in NCR Regional Plan, 2001

centres becomes clear (see Figure 14.2). First, industrial estates have been primarily developed around four National Highways. While there are large differences in the level of development between DMA Towns, industrial estates are being developed in each of them, and of these, Ghaziabad, NOIDA, Faridabad, and Gurgaon play especially important roles as growth centres. On the other hand, most Priority Towns are still not showing results of industrial growth, and whether or not they will function sufficiently as centres for industrial decentralisation and realise balanced NCR growth depends on future development.

As for the reason for regional variances in industrial estate development, it is probably because industrial estate development is not handled by a unified organisation covering all of NCR, but instead by the Industrial Development Corporation of each state. The primary industrial estate development organisations for each state are the DDA and Delhi State Industrial Development Corporation (DSIDC) for Delhi, Haryana Urban Development Authority (HUDA) for Haryana, Rajasthan State Industrial Development & Investment Corporation (RIICO) for

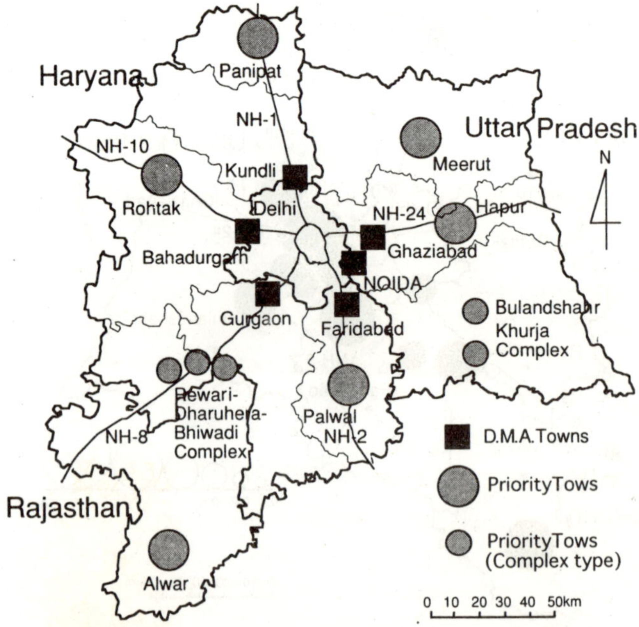

Source: National Capital Region Planning Board[2].

Figure 14.2: Developed area of industrial estates in NCR

Rajasthan, and Uttar Pradesh State Industrial Development Corpocation (UPSIDC) for UP.

These organisations are individually leveraging their proximity to Delhi to develop strategic growth centres. Ghaziabad, NOIDA, and Greater NOIDA are examples of this in UP; for Haryana there are Faridabad and Gurgaon; for Rajasthan, Bhiwadi is closest to Delhi, besides Alwar, which was an industrial agglomeration from early on. All of these are being developed with heavy investment. However, areas in the northeast, north and west of Delhi are lagging in industrial estate development, and as a consequence lopsided development pattern is forming.

INDUSTRIAL ESTATE DEVELOPMENT IN NOIDA: PROCESS AND ADMINISTRATION/OPERATION

NOIDA Development Process

NOIDA lies in the Ghaziabad district of UP (reorganised as Gautam Buddh Nagar district in 1998), and lies to the west of Delhi. NOIDA was originally the name of an industrial estate (and the industrial development corporation responsible for its development); when an industrial estate was developed in Okhla to the immediate west of Delhi, it was christened New Okhla, but as seen above, the abbreviated name of NOIDA came to be widely used as the name of this district.

The UP state government began to develop this area in 1976. Not only industrial areas but also housing, commerce and office spaces were developed. With the addition of physical infrastructure of power, water and sewage, and roads, and social infrastructure such as hospitals (see Figure 14.3), NOIDA began to take the shape of a comprehensive industrial city. The roots of that development can be traced to 1972. In this year, the UP state government fearing that this land near Delhi would be subject to speculative investment, strengthened land trading restrictions. In 1976 it enacted the UP Industrial Area Development law to ensure sustainable development. Based on this, the New Okhla Industrial Development Authority (hereafter referred to as NOIDA Authority) was established as the organisation responsible for overall planned development of this region

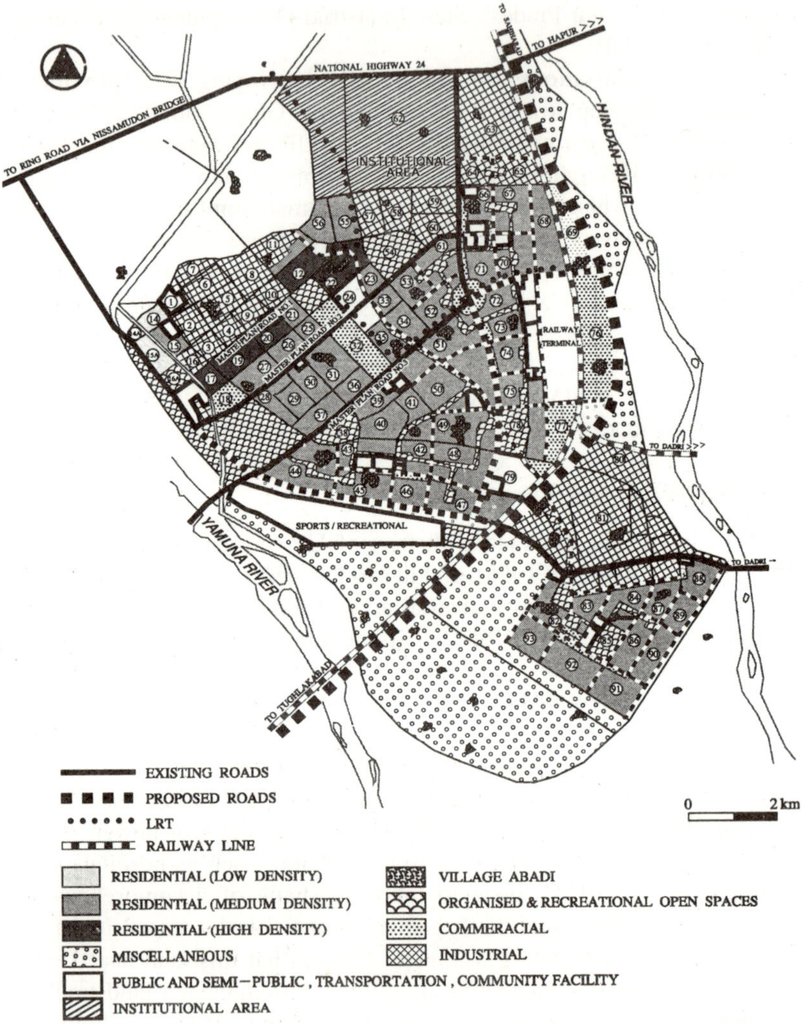

Figure 14.3: Master Plan 2011 of NOIDA

From the beginning, the following four points were the goals of NOIDA development:

1. Decentralise economic activity away from the national capital, and through this reduce the influx of people into Delhi. This would reduce overcrowding in Delhi.

2. Stop speculative land trades that lead to unsustainable/unplanned development.
3. Provide affordable lots near Delhi for relocation of small and medium industries from Delhi and its surroundings.
4. Provide good residential plots at low prices, which cannot be afforded in Delhi.

Even though close to Delhi, because of the Yamuna River, NOIDA was a backward district lagging in urbanisation. For these reasons, with the growth and expansion of the DMA, there was a high risk of speculative development occurring here. NOIDA intended to prevent this speculation, and at the same time take advantage of the low price and easy access to vast lands to develop industrial and residential lots according to a plan, and by doing this create a region that would be a part of the DMA. Of course, from the perspective of UP, which established the developing authority, the intention was to take advantage of the strategic location at the far west of the state, and reduce poverty through growth of the regional economy. Whatever the case, NOIDA is an 'Integrated Industrial Park' which contains not only industries but also residences and other facilities. From the scale of development and conditions, it is appropriate to consider it a planned satellite city of the DMA.

According to the NOIDA Authority, the population was 3,75,000 people in 1997. In the 10 years from 1981 to 1991, the population has grown almost fourfold from 37,000 people to 1,50,000 people, and according to estimated data, reached 2,10,000 people in 1995. Also, according to the master plan, the target population for 2001 was 5,50,000 people and for the 2011 master plan 1.15 million people.

According to the master plan, development area in NOIDA should reach 7,789 ha by 2011. But as of 1997, 3,992 ha, or 50 per cent of the area has already been developed. As for type of land usage, the largest group is residential at 41 per cent, commercial at only 21 per cent. Its characteristic as a region bordering a large city can be seen in its large ratio of residentially zoned land. Also related to this point, the ratio of lots planned for various organisations such as corporate offices, research centres, ITIs, and medical and educational facilities is relatively large.

NOIDA's development plan has been frequently changed, mainly for zoning. Saha & Rao[3] see these changes as (1) an increase of industrial lots due to rezoning, and (2) conversion of agricultural areas to planned areas. Changes (1) can be clearly seen by comparing the master plans for

2001 and 2011, where in response to demand, land zoned for industry has been nearly doubled from 495 ha to 985 ha. The second is the result of conversion to planned areas of places with good accessibility and susceptible to unplanned development. By expanding to the north and east, the planned area has more than doubled in size.

Industrial development, which is the core of NOIDA development, has changed greatly from its original form. During early development, Phase I was for mostly small-scale industries; Phase II was mainly for medium-scale industries, and an Export Processing Zone (NEPZ), of which there are only seven nationwide. Phase III is currently under development, which aims to attract advanced technology industries with its Electronics City and Software Technology Park.

Currently more than 5,500 factories are located in NOIDA. In terms of number of factories (excluding NEPZ), the largest group is socks and clothing with really 20 per cent share. Miscellaneous urban industries, as well as advanced processed industries such as metals and machinery are also concentrated here. This sort of varied industry allows us to view the depth of Delhi's industry and the characteristics of industrial areas near large cities.

Management Characteristics of NOIDA Development

It is worth mentioning that the development of NOIDA was managed and administered solely by the NOIDA Authority. Other states neighbouring Delhi also have overwhelmingly left the work of industrial estate development to these respective Industrial Development Corporations, but their work is extremely limited, involving only development of lots and their sale. None have performed comprehensive urban development which includes development of housing and other facilities. For instance, the new industrial city of Gurgaon in the Delhi suburbs, has no unified authority for land development, and as a result speculative land investment is extremely high, leading to unplanned development.

The following eight functions were specified in the UP State Industrial Area Development law which authorized the establishment of the NOIDA Authority:

1. Acquisition of land for industrial development,
2. Creation of a development plan,
3. Zoning and planning of industrial, commercial and residential lands,
4. Provision of infrastructure for industry, commerce and housing purposes,

5. Provision of amenities,
6. Distribution of industrial, commercial and residential zoned plots through sale or hire,
7. Regulations for structures and factories, and
8. Designation of land for specific purposes.

In order to execute these functions, NOIDA Authority has its own budget. In addition to receiving funds from the state government, it is also empowered to levy taxes for certain purposes. Also, the functions of the NOIDA Authority are not just related to development but extend to a wide range of areas, such as general administration, protection of health, and police. In this way, the single NOIDA Authority encompasses administrative and management functions. But infrastructure for villages within this district, are outside its functions. A similar pattern was seen in the case of MP's Pithampur Industrial Growth Centre. This is a common tendency across India, but it leaves unsolved many problems relating to rural community development.

In fact, the settlements neighbouring NOIDA have many functions not included in the master plan. While housing has been developed according to the plan, it is tended to be occupied by high income earners who commute to Delhi. Most factory workers in NOIDA depend on apartments in these village settlements. Also, commercial facilities developed according to the plan have been brought by luxury goods shops or by property speculators. This has resulted in shops frequented by common folk sprouting up in shopping areas alongside major roads or in the old village areas. Settlements inside the industrial estate are changing to meet new demands, but the living conditions are deteriorating, needing substantial improvement.

As for attracting industry, which is the thrust area of NOIDA development, NOIDA Authority serves many functions. It has actively worked to attract businesses through conveniences such as: 1. a single point of contact, 2. special land pricing, 3. preferential sales of residential lots to incoming companies, 4. sales tax exemption, 5. exemption from power cuts, and 6. easy supply of electricity. For companies desiring to do business in the NCR, this unified response is a great benefit to NOIDA and Greater NOIDA.

Development of Greater NOIDA

Greater NOIDA is situated approximately 15 km southeast of NOIDA, and is an 'IIP' more than five times larger than NOIDA with a

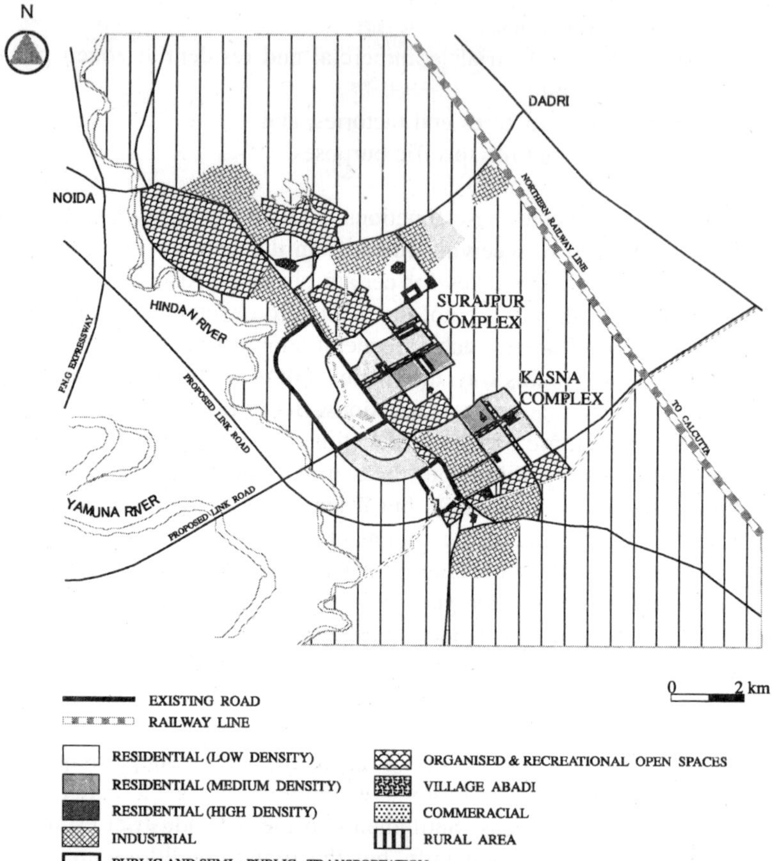

Figure 14.4: Master Plan 2001 of Greater NOIDA

development area of approximately 40,000 ha (see Figure 14.4). Politically, it straddles Dadri tahsil in Ghaziabad district and Sikandarabad tahsil in the Bulandshahr district. Like NOIDA, development of Greater NOIDA was also planned under the UP State Industrial Area Development law. By furthering the development on Surajpur and Kasna industrial estates developed by the UPSIDC, and surrounding areas, the entire region was designated as industrial in 1989, leading to the establishment of the Greater NOIDA Industrial Development Authority in 1991.

The four objectives of Greater NOIDA development are as follows:

1. Avoid unplanned growth and restrict speculative land trades.
2. Within the NCR development policy framework, reduce concentration of population and economic activities in DMA, advance industrial development and integrated, sustainable development.
3. Ensure regional harmony, provide low-density recreation activities.
4. Create industrial employment opportunities, and make it possible to enjoy good working environment and better quality lifestyle.

Here, we see the planned aspect of Greater NOIDA not seen in NOIDA, and which sets it apart in the NCR. Additionally, compared to the relatively older NOIDA, the planning here reveals a strong consideration for comprehensive environmental protection by preserving the river and forests (reserved forests) and by securing open spaces through preserving agricultural lands. Development at Greater NOIDA is notable in aiming for low-density development with a balance of both rural and urban characteristics. It made possible by strong agricultural settlements at the outer edges of the DMA,

Following the economic liberalisation policies of 1991, already 25 foreign firms either have operations here or have plans to do so, and most are large scale. There are four factories covering 20 ha or greater: Honda Ciel Cars India, Escort Yamaha and New Holland Tractor, signifying industrial agglomeration for specialised transportation machinery. Greater NOIDA is a popular destination for foreign companies looking to do business in the NCR.

Let us evaluate Greater NOIDA from the perspective of a company located here, through the case of Honda Ciel Cars India. The company compared Greater NOIDA and Gurgaon (for direct land purchasing) and ultimately chose the former. As reasons for its selection, it cited ease of land acquisition (obtained from the government), land prices (leasing), time required to obtain land, infrastructure (especially power availability), and incentives. Gurgaon came out on top only in the area of safety. The preference for Greater NOIDA is clear from this case. This preference is primarily due to the unified development management method of the Greater NOIDA Authority.

Greater NOIDA, still has many unresolved problems such as social infrastructure, interaction between companies, and incubators. For instance, while factories are moving to Greater NOIDA, no housing developments are being made. Therefore, most factory workers either commute long distances in company buses, or rent apartments in rural settlements inside the district, or rent rooms in farmhouses.

INDUSTRIAL ESTATE DEVELOPMENT ISSUES IN THE NCR

The rise of industrial areas in and around Delhi in recent years has been impressive. This industrialisation has been supported by wide ranging developments across the three states of UP, Haryana and Rajasthan, besides Delhi. But this development has been lopsided occurring in some areas to the south and east of Delhi, like Ghaziabad, Faridabad and Gurgaon. There has not been much development in the Priority Towns, which were intended to be regional growth centres to drive balanced growth across the NCR.

In this chapter, we focused on the core region for industry in Delhi, the IIPs of NOIDA and Greater NOIDA. As growth centres for industrial development in UP, these regions have played an important role until now. After the shift to a liberalised economy in 1991, they have become major agglomerations of foreign firms. These popularity can be attributed to their ability to provide large size lots close to Delhi, and the fact that the developing authority was unified into one public company. Proximity to Delhi made possible large-scale developments. From the perspective of UP, the developing entity, the area was a strategic centre for development and could ease the state's poverty.

However, the hurdles in UP are also plenty, such as frequent changes in political administration and policy, poor provision of electricity, high price for industrial electricity, and long distances from port facilities. The NCR as a whole finds it difficult to attract foreign firms because of problems such as industrial estate development in this region being left up to each state. Using industrial estates as a viable tool for correcting regional disparity, the important policy issues for the future include how to attract foreign firms, and how to handle industrial estate development in the private sector.

NOTES

1 National Capital Regional Planning Board, *National Capital Region: Growth and Development*, New Delhi: Har-Anand Publications, 1996, p. 54.
2 National Capital Regional Planning Board, *National Capital Region: Industrial Potential*, New Delhi: Har-Anand Publications, 1997, pp. 120-35.
3 S.K. Saha and P.S.N. Rao, *NOIDA Surveys 1995: For Revision of Master Plan-2011, Final Report,* New Delhi: School of Planning and Architecture, 1995.

CHAPTER 15

Structure of Industrial Agglomeration in NOIDA and Greater NOIDA: Automobile and Related Industries

KAZUO TOMOZAWA

PROCESS OF INDUSTRIAL AGGLOMERATION AND CHARACTERISTICS OF FACTORIES

NOIDA

First, we will briefly look at industrial plot development in NOIDA as done by the New Okhla Industrial Development Authority. A total of 985 ha was planned to be made available for industrial lots, and as of 1997, already 838 ha had been developed. Spatially, the area is divided into Phase I, Phase II and Phase III (see Figure 15.1). Phase I is the 393 ha developed area bordering Delhi state. Targeting small-scale industries, 4,800 plots were sold in the late 1970s. Taking wind direction into consideration to avoid polluting residential areas with smoke and odours from factories, Phase II was developed at the south-eastern end of the NOIDA area. It is 259 ha in size and its 728 plots were developed for medium-scale industries. The NOIDA Export Processing Zone (NEPZ) created by the Ministry of Commerce and Industry is also situated in Phase II, and many export oriented industries are moving to this zone. Phase III is 206 ha in size with 922 plots. This area was first intended to be developed as residential housing, but due to high demand for industrial plots, its zoning was changed in 1993 and now primarily medium-scale industries are located.

As of March 1997, there were 3,197 small-scale industries and 235 large and medium scale industries in NOIDA. This figure however does not include the 117 factories inside NEPZ (total 12,550 employees, total investment capital Rs. 1.236 billion).

In terms of number of various industries, for ‘hosiery and garments’,

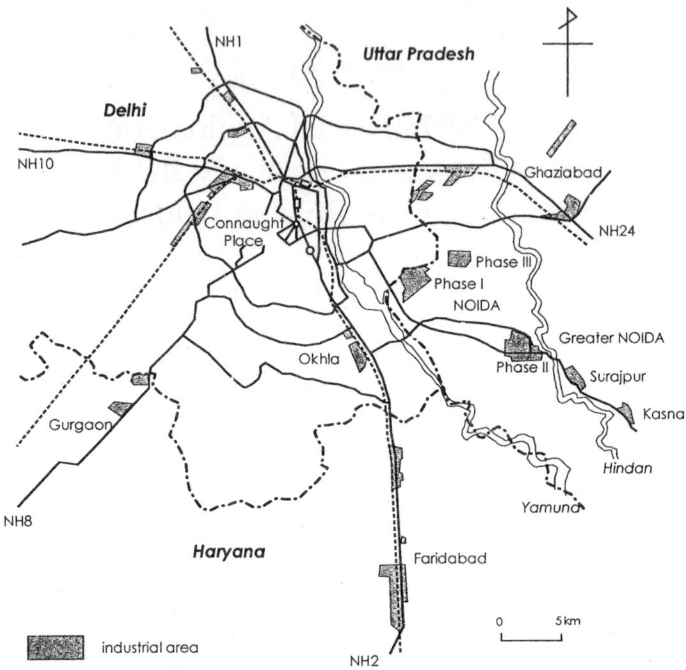

Figure 15.1: Location of NOIDA and Greater NOIDA

'rubber, plastic and petroleum', and 'paper products and printing' comprise more than 10 per cent, indicating that no single industry is predominant (see Table 15.1). The total number of industrial employees in NOIDA is 85,000 people, and only the three sectors of 'hosiery and garments', 'electric machinery and parts' and 'rubber, plastic and petroleum' make up more than 10 per cent of this number.

From the above, we can understand that NOIDA is a comprehensive industrial agglomeration. For transportation equipment belonging to the automobile/automobile related industry, there are 140 factories (4.1 per cent) and 7,352 employees (8.6 per cent). From these numbers, we can say that this industry is not especially prominent at NOIDA, and is just one constituent part of an industrial agglomeration.

Greater NOIDA

Greater NOIDA is an industrial area developed by the Greater NOIDA Industrial Development Authority on 40,000 ha of land about 10-15 km

Table 15.1: Industiries located in NOIDA (1997)

Industry	*No. of factories*	*Investment (Rs. in lakhs)*	*Employment*
Food	52	1,466.15	1,123
Beverage & Tobacco	50	1,042.41	1,442
Cotton textile	42	572.71	864
Jute, hemp & mesta	25	457.58	555
Wool, silk & synthetic	36	947.10	776
Hosiery & garments	663	21,396.95	12,603
Wooden products	89	2,155.40	1,961
Paper products & printing	375	30,852.10	8,398
Leather & leather products	156	16,596.43	2,740
Rubber, plastic & petroleum	474	46,549.57	8,512
Chemical & chemical products	62	3,978.58	3,232
Non-metallic mineral products	38	1,602.01	1,387
Basic metal products	43	2,326.81	1,440
Metal products	99	3,626.67	2,970
Machinery & machine tools	245	16,861.69	8,169
Electric machinery & parts	312	20,196.31	9,872
Transport equipment	140	5,227.08	7,352
Electronic	216	25,522.81	8,037
Others	315	8,231.06	3,567
Total	3,432	209,609.42	85,000

Source: New Okhla Industrial Development Authority.

to the southeast of NOIDA. Surajpur and Kasna industrial complexes form the heart of this industrial development, and by 2001 the former's planned development area was 2,793 ha (of this industrial lots 920 ha) and the latter's was 2,282 ha (676 ha).

Mostly foreign firms are located in this district. As of 1997, 25 foreign factories had moved here or had plans to move here, and together they occupied 332 ha of land and had invested Rs. 6.73 billion. On average, each company had 13.3 ha of land and had invested Rs. 270 million, their scale being significantly larger than the NOIDA regional average (Rs. 6.1 million average investment per factory).

Also, Greater NOIDA is notable for the large number of automakers; 14 of the 25 companies either in business or setting up business here were in the automotive industry: 2 passenger car manufacturers, 1 motor-cycle manufacturer, 1 tractor manufacturer, and 10 component firms. The arrival of complete vehicle producers has sparked the growth of the component market, and this has been a primary driver in making the area the new factory location for component companies.

As seen above, Phase I of NOIDA is for small scale industries, Phase II and III for medium-scale industries, and Greater NOIDA for medium and large industries. Depending on the degree of investment there are differences in factory location. Generally, the further the distance from Delhi, the larger scale the factory is, and here we can surmise that this can be attributed to restrictions on factories near large cities.

LOCATION PROCESS OF AUTOMOBILE MANUFACTURERS AND RELATED INDUSTRIES

Automobile Manufacturers

To learn the characteristics of the automobile industry in this region, we will first understand the factory location strategy and the production climate of complete vehicle manufacturers.

1. ESCORTS YAMAHA MOTOR

This is a joint venture between Escorts and Yamaha. Escorts is headquartered in Delhi, but its production facilities are located in Faridabad, where it has a tractor and two-wheeled vehicle factory. With the deregulation of foreign investment in the 1980s, Escorts formed a technological collaboration with Yamaha for two-wheeled vehicle manufacturing, and established a new 100 cc motorcycle factory at Surajpur. The company cites proximity to Faridabad and incentives as reasons for locating its factory at Surajpur. In 1995, at the request of Escorts, Yamaha took a stake and the Surajpur factory became a joint venture called Escorts Yamaha Motor Limited (EYML). In the following year, two-wheeled vehicle plant came up at Faridabad, making EYML a company with two factories. Intially Escorts and Yamaha held 50 per cent each. From 2000, the capital ratio became 74 for Yamaha versus 26 for Escorts, and the name was also changed to Yamaha Motor Escorts, but for this discussion we use the name at the time of the survey. The company has approximately 4,000 employees, with 3 employees at Faridabad and for each employee at Surajpur. The difference in employee numbers is due to the fact that the former location also includes incidental operations such as R&D functions and customer service department. Both locations build approximately 10,000 motorcycles per month; these are also sent to markets overseas.

2. HONDA SIEL CARS INDIA

Honda Siel Cars India (HSCI) is a joint venture between Honda of Japan and India's Siel Group. Honda owns 60 per cent of the issued stocks and has management control. Founded in 1995 in Kasna, commercial production commenced in December 1997. The company cites proximity to markets, convenient conditions for employee hiring and logistics, and ability to acquire large tracts of continuous land as reasons for locating here, and acknowledges that the location inside the Delhi Capital Region also played a role in its decision. The land is rented from Greater NOIDA Industrial Development Authority for a contracted period of 90 years. It is currently producing the 1,300 cc City, Honda's Asian strategy car, which sells nearly 10,000 units per year.

3. DAEWOO MOTORS INDIA

Daewoo Motors India was located in Surajpur. The process of its foundation and current situation was discussed in Part I; here we will only note its degree of investment. As of 1997 Rs. 3.7 billion had been invested; 55 per cent of this amount had been invested in Greater NOIDA, 4.4 times the investment of HSCI, which also manufacturers passenger vehicles. This indicates the emphasis Daewoo placed on India. It is evident that the objective of this investment was to expand market share.

Automobile Related Industries

According to the telephone book (*NOIDA Yellow Pages*, 1997) there are 60 factories that design and produce components or facilities related to automobile production. Based on this information, we visited each factory, performed interview surveys, and obtained information and data about production and hiring from 24 factories (see Table 15.2).

Of these 24 factories, 19 are located in Phase I and 2 each are located in Phase II and III, and 1 factory in Greater NOIDA. Most companies in Phase I here have a small number of employees and small production values. However, some factories are growing by acquiring neighbouring plots (A-4, A-10). Excluding these, large and medium scale factories are located in Phase II including NEPZ, and in Greater NOIDA.

Surveyed factories cited 'proximity to Delhi' (11 factories) as the important reason for locating here. This can be interpreted to mean enjoyment of various external economies through proximity to the

Table 15.2: Outline of sureyed factories

No.	*Year of establishment*	*Products*	*Employment**	*Turnover** (1996-7)*	*Location*	*Type*
A-1	1979	Filter	43	150	Phase I	Independent
A-2	1982	Sheet metal	8	12	Phase I	Independent
A-3	1984	Starter, wiper	863	12,900	Greater NOIDA	Foreign joint venture
A-4	1984	Wire harness	1,167	11,900	Phase I	Foreign joint venture
A-5	1985	Shaft	21	30	Phase I	Family-owned
A-6	1986	Parts for tractor	29	49	Phase I	Independent
A-7	1986	Forging	73	500	Phase I	Branch factory
A-8	1987	Moulding	355	5,600	Phase II	Branch factory
A-9	1987	Sheet metal	43	150	Phase III	Family-owned
A-10	1988	Rock kits	237	2,855	Phase I	Foreign joint venture
B-1	1980	Parts for machinery	9	8	Phase I	Family-owned
B-2	1993	Parts for clutch	240	345	Phase III	
B-3	1997	Compressor	4	n.a.	Phase I	Independent
C-1	1989	Job work	6	n.a.	Phase I	Family-owned
C-2	1996	Job work	13	n.a.	Phase I	Independent
D-1	1985	Various automobile parts	36	150	Phase I	Branch factory
D-2	1986	Various automobile parts	16	22	Phase I	Family-owned
D-3	1991	Lamps for automobile	1,120	10,003	Phase II	Foreign joint venture
E-1	1979	Load-carrying platform	10	1	Phase I	Family-owned
E-2	1984	Nut	15	n.a.	Phase I	
E-3	1984	Tube valve	28	120	Phase I	Independent
E-4	1985	Assembly of lamp	17	120	Phase I	
F-1	1980	Welding machine	36	166	Phase I	Family-owned
F-2	1986	Testing machine	11	48	Phase I	Independent

Notes: * includes temporary workers;
** Rs. lakhs.
Source: Interviews in each company.

political and economic centres, that is the capital, and orientation to large markets. Six factories placed most emphasis on 'affordable land prices.' Land price in NOIDA in 1978, when development first began, was said to have been Rs. 40 per square metre. This was certainly more affordable than those within the capital. Overall, factories were attracted to this region due to its proximity to the capital region while still having relatively low land prices.

To learn about the formation of agglomeration in NOIDA, we will first understand the management of the surveyed factories (see Table 15.2). The factories can be categorised into foreign joint ventures (A-3, A-4, A-10, D-3) and branch factories of corporations with multiple sites (A-7, A-8, D-2). Both, these types comprise factories with many employ and high values of production. Small-scale factories, can be grouped into following two categories.

The first of these are owned by independents, who launch their own private operations after a working in other companies. Seven factories fall under this category (A-1, A-2, A-6, B-3, C-2, E-3, F-2). After learning about factory management, gaining product technical know-how, entrepreneurs enter into businesses related to their experiences. Except for one factory, these entrepreneurs previously worked in cities near NOIDA such as Delhi and Faridabad.

The second of these groups is factories owned by families, where economic or technical support is provided by parents when the operations are launched, or by launching operations through joint management with siblings or other relatives. Family businesses are common in India. In NOIDA we also found new ventures launched by social groups proficient in the business (such as Sikhs) and businesses where the parents funded their children. However, within the branch factories of corporations with multiple sites, some family-owned businesses have grown to have several factories (A-7, D-2). Excluding these, the remaining factories are one-company, one-factory type operations (A-5, A-9, B-1, C-1, D-1, E-1, F-1). Entrepreneurs belonging to the family-owned category are mainly from Delhi and northern India.

As seen above, it is clear that for establishing automobile-related industries in NOIDA, most large and medium scale enterprises are the result of foreign joint ventures or branch factories of corporations with multiple sites. Small scale factories are managed by entrepreneurs launching new businesses. They are the independent and family-owned types, and there is a close relationship to northern India with regards to place of origin and place of previous employment.

PRODUCTION LINKAGES BETWEEN AUTOMOBILE MANUFACTURERS AND RELATED INDUSTRIES

Trade Structure of Automobile Manufacturers

Here, we discuss the qualities of this industrial agglomeration. For the case studies of HSCI and EYML factories at Surajpur, we look at the component purchasing of full vehicle manufacturers.

HSCI currently has trade agreements with 54 suppliers. From an initial shortlist of over 300 candidate components companies, HSCI picked 54 companies after investigating for about one year on aspects of quality, cost and delivery. The partners include 22 Japanese joint ventures, and in monetary terms this trade comprises 70 per cent of the total. Trade with non-Japanese foreign venture firms accounts for 20 per cent of the trade value, and trade with purely Indian companies accounts for only 10 per cent. The local component acquisition ratio is 50 per cent, but there is likely to be a trend of imported components being slowly replaced by domestic parts. With 70 per cent of trade from Delhi and its surroundings, procurement activities are centred primarily in the capital region.

There are 183 companies handling work outsourced from EYML's Surajpur factory, and in yearly approximately Rs. 1.7 billion worth of components are purchased (see Table 15.3). Outsourcing decisions are made based on cost, delivery, and quality. However, priority is given to components manufactured within the Escorts Group. After the merger with the Faridabad factory, component streamlining and re-evaluation of

Table 15.3: Distribution of suppliers for EYML (1997)

State	*No. of suppliers (%)*	*Share in purchasing (% of cash value)*
Haryana	82 (44.8)	48.6
Uttar Pradesh	20 (10.9)	10.6
Delhi	19 (10.4)	5.5
Tamil Nadu	19 (10.4)	11.1
Maharashtra	17 (9.3)	3.7
Karnataka	11 (6.0)	4.1
Gujarat	5 (2.7)	3.1
Punjab	4 (2.1)	8.2
Others	6 (3.3)	5.1
Total	183 (100.0)	100.0

Souce: Interview from EYML

trade partners are underway to bring about cost reduction. But to avoid risk and additional trouble, the company is adopting a multiple sourcing strategy.

EYML's outsourcing is mainly done within a 50 km radius of the Surajpur factory, and the company purchases from 121 suppliers (64.7 per cent of cash value) based in Haryana, UP and Delhi. The relatively high number of companies from Haryana is due to Escorts' origin in Faridabad, and the historical concentration of related factories of the group having operations in the area. In UP, trade is limited to component companies in NOIDA and Ghaziabad. And like HSCI, procurement activities are centred in the capital region.

Trade Structure of Automobile Related Industries

Next, we will look at the trade relations of component factories. Three layers have been cited in the Indian automotive component industry.

1. the group which supplies original components to automobile manufacturers.
2. the group which provides components for 1.
3. the group which performs component piece processing, called job work.

Automotive factories in Pithampur were categorised into one of 1, 2 or 3, but what is the case for factories in NOIDA?

Table 15.4 shows the locations of the top two customers (in monetary terms) for each surveyed factory. Based on this, we first look at factories vertically integrated into the operations, which have complete vehicle manufacturers at the top of the pyramid.

A: OEM suppliers (A1 to A-10) whose top one or two customers are vehicle manufacturers. They supply original parts on an OEM basis. This was mainly trade with vehicle manufacturers in NCR and Greater NOIDA, or industrial cities in northern India, but some factories also had trade relations with complete vehicle manufacturers in distant Pune (A-1, A-10). By comparing Table 15.4 with Table 15.2, we can see that half of factories belonging to this category are foreign joint ventures and branch factories of corporations with multiple sites. The remainder are relatively small independent and family-owned factories. But there are also some technically advanced factories like A-1 and A-5, which sell components to several complete vehicle manufacturers. Also, it is said that in India there are many niche automotive markets, and if successful in these fields, it is relatively easy to develop trade relations with

Table 15.4: Locations of the top two customers (in monetary terms) for each surveyed factory

No.	Top customer		2nd customer	
	Campany/Type of business (%)	*Location*	*Campany/Type of business (%)*	*Location*
A-1	Maruti Udyog (50)	Gurgaon	TELCO (40)	Pune
A-2	EYML (60)	Greater NOIDA	Parts manufacturer (25)	NOIDA
A-3	Maruti Udyog (63)	Gurgaon	Hero Honda (14)	Dharuhera
A-4	Maruti Udyog	Gurgaon	Honda Siel Cars	NOIDA
A-5	Hero Honda	Dharuhera	Lohia Machines	Kanpur
A-6	Eicher (70)	Alwar	Parts manufacturer (15)	NOIDA
A-7	EYML (15)	Greater NOIDA	Parts manufacturer (11)	NOIDA
A-8	Beverage maker (17)	Delhi	Maruti Udyog (15)	Gurgaon
A-9	EYML (90)	Greater NOIDA	Daewoo (10)	Greater NOIDA
A-10	EYML (25)	Greater NOIDA	Bajaj Auto (20)	Pune
B-1	Parts manufacturer		Parts manufacturer	NOIDA
B-2	Parts manufacturer	Faridabad	Parts manufacturer	Aurangabad
B-3	Flex	NOIDA	Parts manufacturer	NOIDA
C-1	Parts manufacturer	NOIDA	Parts manufacturer	NOIDA
C-2	Parts manufacturer	Delhi	Parts manufacturer	NOIDA
D-1	Parts trader (10)	Jordan	Parts trader (10)	Saudi Arabia
D-2	Parts trader	Southeast Asia		
D-3	Parts trader	Luxembourg	Parts trader	Canada
E-1	Parts trader	Delhi	Parts trader	Delhi
E-2	Parts trader	NOIDA	Parts trader	NOIDA
E-3	Parts trader	Lucknow	Parts trader	Pune
E-4	Parts trader	Delhi	Parts trader	Delhi
F-2	TELCO	Jamshedpur	Maruti Udyog	Gurgaon

Source: Interviewed from each companies

complete vehicle manufacturers. A-2, A-6 and A-9 are examples of this.

B: Secondary supplier types (B-1 to B-3) are factories that supply components to OEM suppliers. Their customers are primarily in NOIDA and nearby industrial cities.

C: Job work types (C-1, C-2) receive simple piece work components. The piece rate is cheap, and there is large variability in volume, so this is the least economically stable type. C-1 is a business founded by brothers to as a way out of agriculture, and lacking in management and technical know-how, the business is currently suffering financial difficulties.

As seen above, there are many companies that are integrated into the operations of complete vehicle manufacturers mainly in the Delhi capital region. But on the other hand it is evident that there are also automotive factories without these trade relations.

D: Exporters (D-1to D-3) are companies that perform component manufacture for overseas markets. D-1 exports all of its production to the Middle East and Southeast Asia. However, it planned to begin trade with domestic complete vehicle manufacturers from 1998. D-2 exports products throughout Southeast Asia through a trade company run by the owner's father. At first, it supplied OEM parts to domestic automakers, but shifted to exports in 1992 in pursuit of greater profit margins. D-3 is obligated to export due to its location in NPEZ. It manufactures automotive lamps and exports 75 per cent of its production, and the remainder are delivered to domestic automakers.

E: Repair parts type companies (E-1 to E-4) manufacture parts for the after-market and ship products directly to parts dealers for sale to end consumers. Parts produced by these factories are not used as OEM parts by full vehicle manufacturers, and have relatively low price points. Following the recent growth of the automobile market, the after-market parts sector has been also growing, and these factories are showing increased sales across the board.

F: Manufacturing equipment developers (F-1, F-2) are small-scale industries with R&D capabilities that accept orders for equipments in automobile factory assembly lines. F-2 manufactures various types of testing equipment and usually delivers one to two months after an order is placed. It has few competitors and says business is going well.

The trading pattern of the automotive related factories in NOIDA as described above is summarised in Figure 15.2. In addition to factories vertically integrated into the operations of full vehicle manufacturers, factories of exporters are located in NOIDA for convenience in ex-

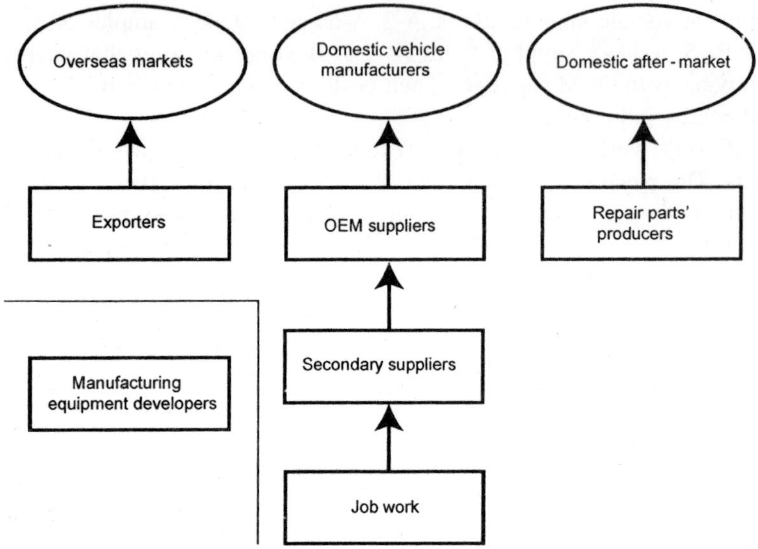

Figure 15.2: Trading pattern of automotive-related factories in NOIDA

porting. There are also the repair parts factories that produce to meet the special needs of urban markets. Then, there were small-scale factories developing manufacturing equipment.

DIFFERENCES IN INDUSTRIAL AGGLOMERATION BETWEEN NOIDA, GREATER NOIDA AND PITHAMPUR

In this chapter, by taking NOIDA and Greater NOIDA as case studies for the automotive industry we learned about the process of factory site selection and production linkages for industrial estates in the capital region of Delhi. By doing this, together with the study of the Pithampur Industrial Growth Centre discussed in Chapter 9, we were able to understand the regional structure of the two automobile industry locations types: backward districts and those at the outer edge of existing economic centrs. Finally, while the comparing characteristics of both the regions, we would like to summarise our findings.

NOIDA has the advantage of urban markets due to its location inside NCR and proximity to Delhi. Even now complete vehicle manufacturers flow into the area. On the other hand, Pithampur is an industrial growth centre developed in a backward district, and its advantages are limited to special incentives and cheap land. In the 1980s four automakers started operations there, but since the 1990s no new entrants have been seen. Instead there have been instances of foreign investment partners pulling out of ventures formed here. In the 1990s interference of government into business site selection was lessened, which allowed businesses to choose location based on economic merits. But more than merits afforded by locating in backward districts, complete vehicle manufacturers valued on the various benefits that could be obtained in urban areas.

Major differences were also seen between the two types of regions on the point of trade relations with complete vehicle manufactures. In Pithampur, complete vehicle manufacturers relied more on existing centres of industry in other states for their component supplies, and trade with local partners was limited to only about 20 per cent of the total. On the other hand, in Greater NOIDA, trade within the capital region accounted for nearly all component supply, and purchasing of components from distant states was unusual. Proximity to the supply location was far more important for NOIDA and this is surmised to greatly impact (positively) production costs.

For automotive related factories, there was a clear difference found in viability. In Pithampur, the only automotive related factories were local ones that moved to Pithampur to capture business from complete vehicle manufacturers, their move coinciding with the latter's arrival in Pithampur. The two were formed a localised integrated structure in which complete vehicle manufacturers came at the top of the production chain. On the other hand, in the case of NOIDA we can find a more varied composition. Trade partners for OEM suppliers were not just assembly plants in Greater NOIDA, but also included several automakers in the capital region. Also, there were factories aiming at overseas markets and the after-market, as well as factories developing equipment for use in assembly lines, which showed that the structure of viability is more diverse, and the spatial spread of trade relationships is great.

In this way, when looking at the automobile industry, the timing of development of these industrial agglomerations is similar, but there are large qualitative differences attributed to their geographical locations.

CHAPTER 16

Housing Development and Dweller Characteristics

YOSHIMICHI YUI

URBAN PLANNING IN THE NATIONAL CAPITAL REGION

Even after independence, private investment in India has been concentrated in urbanised areas. Of these urbanised areas, from its role simply as a political city, Delhi began to emerge as an economic centre. Large increases in population due to migration from rural villages. Together with the refugees, large-scale migration, causing further worsening of urban issues. For this reason, issues such as plans to redevelop Delhi and handling of urban problems after the Third Five Year Plan were to be addressed by the central government. Furthermore, urban redevelopment plans for many cities implemented by the mid-1960s.

Also, industry location policies were formed to decentralise population and industry that had become concentrated in large cities. A decentralisation strategy was formed to encourage license factories in local regions for not only primary industry but private industry as well. Many tax incentives and other benefits were provided for factories in backward districts. However, even though there are less policy incentives to be enjoyed than backward districts. In addition to industry moving into metropolitan suburban areas from metropolitan inner areas, many new factories and venture firms funded with foreign capital were taking advantage of existing industrial agglomerations. As a result, industrial concentration continues in metropolitan areas.

In the capital region of Delhi, Faridabad and Gurgaon were built to reduce industry and population density. Established in 1955, the DDA put forward the Delhi Development Act and announced a Master Plan for Delhi in 1962. According to this plan, six cities including Gurgaon were designated as Ring Towns, and to reduce the population density of Delhi, factories were actively encouraged to move here.

NOIDA, bordering Delhi to the east, is not a Ring Town, but like towns such as Gurgaon, was designated as a DMA town.[1] Due to preferential policies for small-scale industry from the late 1960s, small and medium scale factories moved from inner-city of Delhi to NOIDA, and development is continuing on "Integrated Industrial Parks" that combine work and residential infrastructures.

With economic liberalisation policies of the 1980s, NOIDA grew into a mammoth industrial estate through the appearance of large-scale factories funded with foreign capital. NOIDA succeeded in doing this by taking advantage of existing industrial agglomerations and skilled workforce to provide excellent business conditions for foreign corporations. Interviews with the staff of Japanese companies in NOIDA, revealed that for staff class workers and their families relocating from Japan, the proximity to the capital Delhi not just made for a convenient lifestyle but was especially advantages for dealing with problem situations or getting in contact with Japan.

Through a case study of NOIDA, built as part of an urban development plan in the capital region, and studying the quality of residents in its housing colonies, this chapter analyses housing supply in India based on urban planning.

DEVELOPMENT OF HOUSING IN NOIDA

Development of NOIDA

In India, typically the Housing Board of each state is responsible for housing supply, but at NOIDA the Housing Bureau within the Authority is responsible for the housing supply. This is because NOIDA Authority is the organisation with overall jurisdiction over development in the area, and it fulfils unified functions include provision of infrastructure, supply of industrial and housing lots, as well as the construction and sale of housing.

According to the original Master Plan, 49.2 per cent of the total area was zoned residential, revealing the equal importance the plan gave to incoming industry and suburban housing. Also, the residential land was subdivided, with homes for high-level government bureaucrats and upscale housing located in the areas closest to Delhi, and small and medium-scale factories moving from Delhi concentrated in the northern sectors. Additionally, high density housing bordered the industrial districts, and low density residential districts were located in the peripheral sectors. Commercial areas were located in the west, and large-scale commercial agglomerations are still being built.

According to the Master Plan, NOIDA's total developed area was 7,789 ha and the planned population in 2001 was 5,50,000 people. In 2011 the population was planned to reach 1.15 million people, but due to delays in provision of housing, as of October 1997, the population is approximately 3,75,000 people. Table 16.1 shows the zoning changes between the original Master Plan 2001 and the revised Master Plan 2011, and actual land usage as of 1997. While 3,672 ha of residential area and approximately 30,000 units were planned, as of October 1997, housing units built directly by NOIDA only reached approximately half of the target, 14,602 units. An additional, 14,625 residential lots were made available for sale to owners who would arrange for their own home construction. There are also industrial lots and apartments for sale to families of public sector workers inside the residential sectors.

Table 16.1: Land use plans and present conditions

Land uses	*Master Plan 2001*		*Master Plan 2011*		*Land use existing in 1995*	
	Area (ha)	*%*	*Area (ha)*	*%*	*Area (ha)*	*%*
Residential	1,870	49.2	3,672	47.14	1,131	42.15
Industrial	495	13	985	12.65	811	30.23
Commercial	230	6.1	431	5.53	132	4.92
Public and semi-public	365	9.6	1,224	15.71	92	3.40
Transportation	495	13	941	12.08	365	13.60
Organised open spaces	292	7.7	536	6.89	152	5.70
Unusable land-water bodies	53	1.4	0	0.00	0	0.00
Total	3,800	100.0	7,789	100.00	2,683	100.00

Sources: 'Master Plan 2001', 'Master Plan 2011', and S.K. Saha and P.S.N. Rao.[2]

As the government of Haryana encouraged housing supply through quick land development with private capital, urban planning in Gurgaon has attracted sizable investment. Inside Delhi, on the other hand, the DDA has taken up purchase, development and clearance for large tracts of land, frozen development on private land, and shifted the distribution arrangements for developed land from purchasing to leasing contracts. Like Delhi, NOIDA Authority also holds a complete monopoly over land purchasing, development and sales, and controls urban development. As a result, even though it borders Delhi, the pace of development outside the central area is slow.

Current Land Usage Situation

When a comparison of current land usage of NOIDA is compared to the plan for Phase I, the first stage of development planning, it is apparent that development has largely followed the Master Plan. As shown in Figure 16.1, areas planned for industrial lots in central NOIDA are basically the same as in the Master Plan, but to encourage foreign industrial investment residential areas Master Plan 2001 have been converted into industrial areas. The new NEPZ district has also reduced residential area. Additionally, there are still many empty lots in the peripheral sectors, and housing construction here has begun only recently. According to Saha and Rao,[3] 80 per cent of the planned industrial lots have been developed, but only 30 per cent of the planned residential lots have been developed.

Medium and high-rise corporate housing residential blocks for government-linked companies are being constructed in peripheral sectors where medium-density housing is planned. Of these, housing complexes built in the 1980s in Sector 55 are company housing for public sector workers employed in Delhi. Interviews with the company housing management office revealed that, residents of the area board three charter buses at 8:20 in the morning to commute to Delhi. Nearly all residents own scooters and some own cars, but these are not used for commuting to work. There are small shopping centres in these large company housing complexes, but residents shop at central NOIDA or in Harola or Atta villages, which existed before the development of NOIDA but have since transformed into commercial agglomerations.

Large number of housing units for army personnel are provided in conveniently located sectors. With wide town houses, medium density housing and high-rise housing are provided depending on the rank of the army personnel, and separated by sector.

Land prices are skyrocketing in planned residential sectors. Prices have shot up approximately tenfold since development began in 1985 until the time of the survey, November 1997. Also, there are large differences in prices between sectors. In Sector 15A, which is near Delhi (see Figure 16.1), the purchase price for 1 sq m is between Rs. 25,000 and 30,000 and in sectors such as Sectors 14, 17, 19, 26, 27 and 30, the same 1 sq m costs between Rs. 15,000 and 18,000. Businessmen, government officials, and public sector workers live in these sectors.

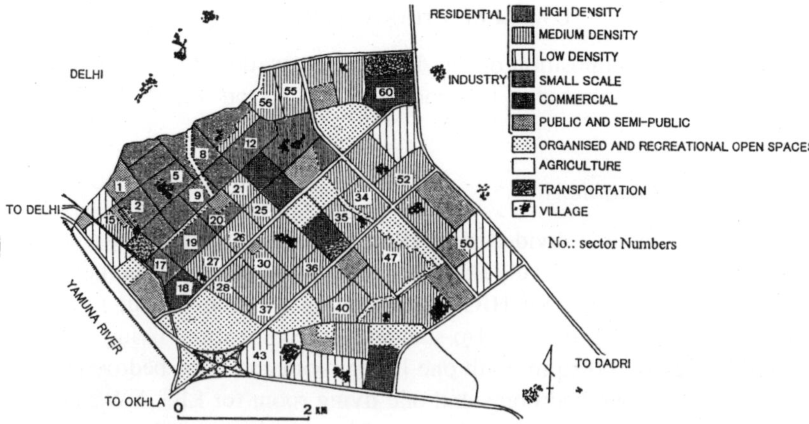

Source: 'Master Plan NOIDA 2001' and Field Research in 1997.

Figure 16.1: Land use plan for NOIDA

On the other hand, eastern and northern sectors surrounding built up areas are even lower priced, with 1 sq m of land going for under Rs. 8,000. But prices are starting to skyrocket here as well. Due to the distance from central area of NOIDA and mosquito increase due to salt contained in the groundwater, the land prices in these peripheral areas were lower when compared with other sectors. However, the Rs. 1,300 per sq m price of around 1995 had increased to Rs. 7,000 per sq m as of December 1997, taking it out of the reach of the middle class.

As reported by Saha and Rao,[4] factory workers moving to the suburbs are living in villages that exist inside NOIDA but are left out of its development. For most factory line workers, purchasing homes in NOIDA is economically difficult, and they end up staying in rental housing managed by the landowner class in the urban villages.

Large-scale slums stretch out to the west of the drainage canal in Sector 17 and in empty spaces underneath high voltage power lines in Sectors 8 and 9. This spread of slum is a common characteristic all over India, but slums are not seen in industrial districts. This is due to the fact that slum dwellers are mostly factory construction workers or factory cleaning workers, or cleaners of public facilities or luxury homes. In other words, slum dwellers are not workers directly involved in the line work of factories, but labourers indirectly affected by industrialisation.

DWELLER CHARACTERISTICS

To konw the composition of the dwelling types, door-to-door interview surveys were conducted in December 1997 in Sectors 12, 15, 17, 19 and 36.

Residential Conditions

Housing in India is divided into: HIG, MIG, LIG and EWS categories, according to income level. There is a significant difference in the living area for each group; for HIG residences, in addition to four rooms, a room for a live-in maid is also standard. In NOIDA, the living area for HIG homes is 100 sq m, with one living room and three bedrooms, 60-80 sq m with two bedrooms and one living room for LIG, EWS homes have a single with an area 22-25 sq m. There are plenty of HIG and MIG houses in at NOIDA but few EWS homes for industrial labourers because those areas have been rezoned for industrial use.

In the surveyed sectors, most plots for sale were in MIG and LIG categories, but approximately 30 per cent of these are now available as rental properties. The majority of HIG plots, on the other hand, are owned by their residents.

In terms of household income for each residence type, while LIG residents are mostly low-income earners making Rs. 5,000-9,999 per month, most MIG households earn more than Rs. 10,000 per month. Also, Saha and Raos clarified that 16 per cent of those earned more than Rs. 15,000 per month,[5] luxury homes are also included. We expected a clear difference in living standards with differences in income, but in reality high-income earners also occupy LIG residences, and the type of residence is not necessarily related to the income level of its occupants.

According to residents, for Sector 55, rents for company housing for public corporations and public workers account for about 30 per cent of their income. Also, according to real estate companies and residents, houses for military families is provided according to rank, with monthly rent for a two room unit ranging from Rs. 950-1,499. Houses for military families are also subleased to non-military personnel, with two bedroom units being rented for about Rs. 4,000-5,000, three bedroom units for about Rs. 10,000, and 12,000-14,000 for a four bedroom units.

In terms of household amenities, since all units have toilets and showers, residents are more satisfied here than in their previous places of living. There is a difference in automobile ownership between HIG and MIG residents, and in terms of colour televisions, there is a difference found between public housing and LIG homes. Most households have refrigerators, highlighting the difference between high and low income groups in regional cities. Other than HIG, few residents owned air-conditioners.

Age and Family Structure

Most heads of LIG homes are young, while for MIG, HIG and houses built on plots of similar size, the householders' age is higher (see Table 16.2). In terms of location, LIG homes in Sector 12, relatively far from the central areas, have heads in their early thirties, While in Sector 19, they are in thirties and early forties. The age of head of household for MIG and HIG homes is higher, with many in their forties and fifties. Additionally, in Sector 17, comprising of five storey blocks of company housing for BHEL and most heads of household are in the forties age range. In this company housing block, interaction was seen between different *jati*, where housewives would meet and knit even with members of different *jati*.

Family structure for the majority of households was relatively young in their thirties and forties, and 62.4 per cent were nuclear families with parents and children. For joint families (living together with families of multiple siblings and parents) thought to be numerous in UP, Saha and Rao[6] report high percentages, but our results only found 8 joint families. Meanwhile, the reason there are few single men even though this is a region where factories have opened up is thought to be because NOIDA is a satellite city with strong qualities of being oriented toward families. Also, hardly any single factory workers live in the typical housing areas such as those targeted for the surveyed sectors, and instead live in rented housing in villages.

Table 16.2: Age structure of householders by housing types

	Age of householders									
Housing types	*20-4*	*25-9*	*30-4*	*35-9*	*40-4*	*45-9*	*50-4*	*55-9*	*60-*	*Total*
GOVT. FLATS	0	0	1	1	2	0	0	1	0	5
LIG	0	2	11	10	11	5	2	0	3	44
MIG	0	5	7	3	4	15	10	1	7	52
PLOT (except HIG or MIG size)	1	1	2	6	4	2	3	2	5	26
PLOT(HIG size)	0	0	0	2	0	0	1	1	1	5
PLOT(MIG size)	0	0	0	0	1	0	0	0	0	1
Total	1	8	21	22	22	22	16	5	16	133

Source: Field Survey in 1997.

Occupation and Educational Background

Most heads of household are factory managers or public workers. The high number of public workers is due to the fact that they work in government-affiliated public companies. The high number large of high income residents at NOIDA is related to the fact that most heads of households are from upper castes and have university or higher education. Also, the educational level of the spouses of many heads of households is high, with many having university or higher level of education.

MOVEMENT OF PLACE OF RESIDENCE

In terns of the place of birth of the head of the household, 47 (35.3 per cent) were from UP., 27 (20.3 per cent) were from Delhi, followed by Haryana state. Most were thus born in nearby states.

When comparing head of household's last level of education and birthplace, while nearly half from UP had graduated university degrees or more, 80 per cent of those from Delhi had completed university or higher education. This highly educated segment is made up of employees commuting to Delhi, and they are not necessarily involved with industrial development of NOIDA. In addition, the ratio of heads of household from states such as Punjab and Kerala who have completed junior school is high.

More than half of those from Delhi live in HIG and MIG plots the well to do, while those from Kerala and UP live in varied residences, many in LIG areas. All residents of public housing were from UP.

Next, for relation between previous place of residence and birthplace, most people from Delhi had previously lived in Delhi. More than a third of respondents said that they were born outside of UP and arrived in NOIDA after having lived in Delhi. This reveals that NOIDA performs its role of a satellite city in the suburbs of Delhi.

Residents' Evaluation of Lifestyle

The majority of residents were satisfied with the life in NOIDA, giving especially high marks to the lack of pollution and absence of water shortages. Rather than reflection of the good living conditions at NOIDA, there are thought to be a relative evaluations by former Delhi residents of the pollution issues of Delhi. Also, the suburban lifestyle itself is highly praised. The appeal of living in new suburb away from busy cities, together with an investment in real estate, is evoking rapid suburbanisation in India.

On the other hand, many residents were unsatisfied with the power supply, due to frequent power outages. Also, many complained about lack of roads, rail existing in only plans, frequent traffic jams due to increased number of cars, and the long commute time to Delhi. There were also worries about public safety due to the mass influx of newcomers. Violent crimes such as robberies and kidnappings were said to be on the rise in the high-income sectors, especially. Emerging problems drainage during the monsoon season, sanitary concerns such as high number of mosquitoes and flies, and untimely response to demand for housing for workers at new factories.

Additionally, there was dissatisfaction with the monotony of life. Each sector is planned to be made up of various housing types, and through this a mixed development model is used with the goal of increasing variety of social classes of residents. However, in reality, the society is formed only of the well off, mostly from the middle and upper classes. For instance, while housing in each sector is varied, the previous place residence provided a much more varied society.

URBAN PLANNING ISSUES IN NOIDA

Development in NOIDA is handled by the NOIDA Authority, which is responsible for planning and supply. On this point, while there are benefits of unified land planning, housing supply, and provision of infrastructure, the development plan itself has undergone various changes and lacks consistency. Such changes seem to be common in Delhi's urban planning as well but in this area, impacted by complex political power relationships, is a special characteristic. Also, due to the different jurisdictions, a unified infrastructure plan has not been made even though there is a close relationship with Delhi capital region.

Though NOIDA's development is managed by a single developing entity, delays and administration issues are emerging. Especially, in over 50 villages in the developed area, where there is no investment from the developer for roads, water, sewage or other infrastructure. With the influx of factory workers into these settlements, they are becoming more overcrowded. Suburban development like that being done at NOIDA is not growing like urban redevelopment inside Delhi due not only to issues of cost but also as a result of development methods unique to India, where improvements are not made to village areas, instead these areas are left out of the urban development activities.

The original objective of developing a highly independent and self-sustaining city had changed. From serving as a location for small and medium factories from Delhi to move for the purpose of decentralisation, NOIDA is today growing large scale factories by enticing foreign firms. Furthermore, with an increasing ratio of housing supply for workers commuting to Delhi, the region can be called a satellite city of Delhi. Related to this point, Saha, who studied urban planning in NOIDA, says that NOIDA functions as a part of Delhi, but because politically it is a special district of UP, from the early planning stages, it has been an urban development that remains dependent upon Delhi.

NOTES

1 National Capital Regional Planning Board, *National Capital Region: Growth and Development*, New Delhi: Har-Anand Publications, 1996.
2 S.K. Saha and P.S.N. Rao, *NOIDA Surveys 1995: For Revision of Master Plan-2011, Final Report,* New Delhi: School of Planning and Architecture, 1995.
3 Ibid.
4 Ibid.
5 Ibid.
6 Ibid.

CHAPTER 17

Commercial Centres: Formation and Characteristics

HIROKAZU SAKUNO

COMMERCIAL CENTRES WITH DIFFERING ORIGINS

An estimated agglomeration of 5,50,000 people was expected to be concentrated in NOIDA in 2001, and commercial facilities were planned to meet the inevitable demand for commerce. When complete, a relatively high 15.8 per cent of land area is planned for commercial use, revealing the emphasis placed on city functions. These commercial facilities can be thought of as planned to be distributed throughout NOIDA.

While land has been set aside for Town Centres (Sector 25A, 32), as of 1997, these remain as large open spaces with commercial agglomerations being all but missing. However, Sub-District Centre (Sector 18) is already a dedicated commercial sector with retail buildings selling luxury goods, office buildings, movie theatres, hotels, and fast food restaurants. These Town Centres and Sub-District Centres are supplying high-level goods and services for the entire NOIDA area.

Additionally, supplementing these abovementioned commercial sectors, every sector has a large scale shopping centre. Currently, there is the Gulmohar Shopping Centre in Sector 15 and the Ganga Shopping Centre in Sector 28. For both of these shopping centres, various tenant are doing business in shopping buildings constructed by the NOIDA Authority. There are also super bazaars, which follow the same format but on a relatively smaller scale. Furthermore, a Sector Shop has been placed in each residential sector, and there are Convenient Shops in sectors covering greater areas.

Summing up the planned placement of commercial facilities, the NOIDA Authority proposes three types of commercial facilities. These are Town Centres, serving all of NOIDA, Sub District Centres which are are at the next, and in some sectors there are shopping centres and super bazaars which supplement these. Additionally for each sector, there are Sector Shops and Convenient Shops.

In this way, a system has been created in NOIDA that hierarchically supplies goods and services across the entire industrial estate. For most of the Sectors 1-40 which have already been developed, Sector Shops or Convenient Shops have been set up, and for the commercial Sector 18 there is an ongoing agglomeration of shops and offices. It is not a stretch to say that planned commercial centres are taking shape.

Incidentally, through planned placement of widened roads and zoning along sector units for land usage as shown in the Figure 17.1, the goal is for NOIDA to be an integral industrial estate with a very high level of detailed planning. Also, infrastructure needed for industrial production and residences such as electricity, water and sewage are complete. However, spread throughout the industrial estate like islands, the existence of approximately 40 rural settlements is odd, especially given the high degree of land usage and facility planning that has been done.

These rural settlements existed before the development of NOIDA. Currently undeveloped areas and portions planned to be left as farmland even in the 2011 plan retain their traditional rural landscape. However, for areas already developed into industrial estates, even though their surroundings have been transformed into industrial and residential plots, the rural settlements continue to exist as such. These settlements are represented in the development plans as blank areas, and treated as areas which will not be touched by development. Also, infrastructure such as road, sewage and water are not provided at all, and living conditions are very bad.

This type of development is thought to be highly unusual, but in India similar cases can be found in Gurgaon and Faridabad. In NOIDA as in the other two towns, the roads have been clearly planned to not cut across rural settlements. At first, the intention appears to be protect these rural settlements, but due to the lack of integrated infrastructure, this could also be viewed as development that is ignoring rural settlements. Meanwhile, the villages will lose their surrounding farmland once development is complete, ceasing to function as agricultural communities.

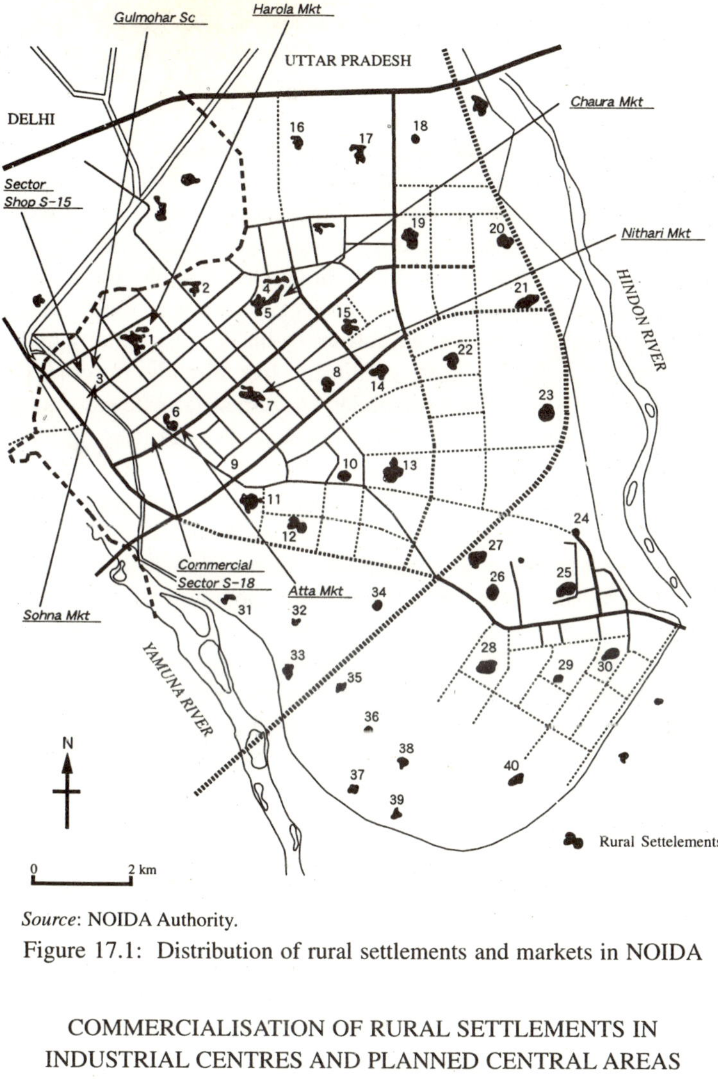

Source: NOIDA Authority.

Figure 17.1: Distribution of rural settlements and markets in NOIDA

COMMERCIALISATION OF RURAL SETTLEMENTS IN INDUSTRIAL CENTRES AND PLANNED CENTRAL AREAS

The placement of residential facilities within an industrial estate is intended to provide places of residence for workers who work at factories inside the industrial estate. However, the supply of high density residential properties appropriate for factory labourers is limited in NOIDA, with most housing being low to medium density residential plots.

Plot types in sectors are determined by the NOIDA Authority and single-family homes and apartment-style multiple dwellings have been built in most residential sectors. Consequently, housing facilities are not provided for low income workers who cannot afford to own homes, or for single labourers who do not require home ownership. It is the rural settlements that meet this demand by renting out rooms in farm houses or building rental dwellings on their properties. Many factory workers employed at NOIDA commute from nearby villages, but more live within these rural settlements. Many households employed at NOIDA live in residential sectors, but due to its proximity to Delhi, the percentage of residents who commute from Delhi is exceptionally high.

Incidentally, the NOIDA Authority has already purchased the farmland of most villages surrounded by industrial estates, making it virtually impossible for rural village residents to engage in agricultural activities. As a result, the original residents of these rural settlements have begun finding employment in professions other than agriculture. In addition to working in factories in the industrial estate, they have tried their hand in various new occupations, such as entering into the real estate market using their land as capital, or opening retail shops on land inside and outside the rural settlements. By opening retail shops to meet the demand of relatively low-income buyers living in these villages, the rural settlements have been slowly transformed into commercial centres.

Also, planned commercial facilities have been placed by the NOIDA Authority in each sector. As a result, two types of central areas have come to coexist in NOIDA–commercial centres developed through planned placement of commercial facilities and central areas spontaneously emerging in changing rural settlements. Referring to the former as 'planned central areas', and the latter as 'spontaneous central areas', the next section seeks to understand the site characteristics of both types of areas.

SITE CHARACTERISTICS OF SHOPS AND OFFICES IN COMMERCIAL CENTRES

To reveal the differences in scale and function between planned and spontaneous central areas in NOIDA industrial estates, we calculated the number of shops and offices from the telephone book. Here, the term 'shops' refers to facilities that provide goods or services from a storefront. Home appliance, motorcycle and bicycle repair shops are also included in this category. Additionally, tabulation of offices was limited to those which had permanently staffed front desks and were set up to provide services in person. These conditions resulted in most counted offices being real estate businesses; establishments that only provided administrative functions for companies were not included. While not technically offices, banks and clinics that play important central functions were also added to this count.

Shown in Table 17.1 is the tally of shops and offices for primary commercial centres of each sector. The results show that there were 12 central areas in Sectors 1-40, which were analysed here, and of these, 5 were planned central areas and 7 are spontaneous central areas. Eight rural settlements can be found from Sectors 1-40, and excepting one village, all have turned into commercial centres. Each of these villages has over 100 shops and offices, and of these Atta and Harola are especially large, followed by Naya Bans, Nithari, and Chaura.

On the other hand, looking at sectors with planned central areas, the most shops and offices are found in Sector 15 in the Gulmohar Shopping Centre. Naya Bans, a spontaneous central area, is also situated in this sector. The large number of shops and offices in Sector 15 is not solely attributable to the presence of Gulmohar Shopping Centre. While there are over 200 shops and offices, this number is equal to or less than sectors with spontaneous central areas. In this way, in terms of number of shops and offices, we can say that spontaneous central areas are larger in scale than planned central areas.

Table 17.2 details shops and offices found in this survey, categorised according to type of business, and it shows the count for each primary central area. Accordingly, we can say that in terms of shops and offices overall, Harola and Atta are approximately the same size. In Harola, together with a prevalence of electrical components, the number of household appliances, machinery repair businesses and real estate offices is also notable. On the other hand, in Atta, high-level goods and service functions are prominent, such as shops offering ready to wear clothing, restaurants, service offices, and financial/medical services. Considering its location next to commercial Sector 18, which deals in luxury goods, Atta is understood to be a relatively high-order commercial centre, and low-order goods and services are supplied around Harola, showing a natural functional separation. On the other hand, there are substantially less shops in planned central areas than in spontaneous central areas. For instance, with 114 shops and offices, Sector 18 is the largest of planned

Table 17.1: The number of shopping zone and shops in each sector in NOIDA (1997)

Sector No.	Land Use Plan by Master Plan 2011	No. of Shopping Zone: Plan: Sector Shop	Convenient Shop	Complete	No. of Shops or Offices*	Main Market Name
1	Industrial	1	1	1	35	
2	Industrial	–	–	–	63	
3	Industrial	–	–	2	50	
4	Industrial	–	–	–	64	
5	Industrial	–	–	–	477	Harola Market
6	Industrial	1	–	1	66	
7	Industrial	–	–	–	52	
8	Industrial	–	–	–	40	
9	Industrial	–	–	–	245	
10	Industrial	–	–	–	144	
11	Industrial & Residential	1	1	1	199	Jhundpura Market
12	Residential	8	–	7	338	
14	Residential	1	–	1	31	
14A	Residential	1	–	–	–	
15	Residential	1	1	3	327	Sohna (Naya Bans) Market, Gulmohar Shopping Center
15A	Residential	1	–	2	–	Super Bazaar
16	Industrial	–	–	1	61	
16A	Public	–	–	–	–	
17	Residential	–	1	1	26	
18	Commercial	1	–	1	242	Commercial Sector
19	Residential	1	–	3	231	
20	Residential	1	3	1	140	Super Bazaar
21	Residential	–	–	2	224	
21A	Open space	–	–	–	–	
22	Residential	2	–	3	278	Chaura (Sadatpur, Raghunathpur) Market
23	Residential	1	2	–	8	
24	Public	–	–	–	2	
25	Residential	–	–	–	218	
25A	Commercial	–	–	–	–	
26	Residential	2	–	1	121	
27	Residential	2	–	2	779	Atta Market
28	Residential	–	–	1	152	
29	Residential	–	–	2	243	Ganga Shopping Center
30	Residential	1	–	–	49	
31	Residential	2	–	2	305	Nithari Market
32	Commercial	–	–	–	5	
33	Residential	1	1	–	7	
34	Residential	1	3	3	96	
35	Residential	1	–	–	–	
36	Residential	–	4	–	30	
37	Residential	1	1	3	197	Harijan Basti Market
38	Open space	–	–	–	2	
39	Residential	1	2	3	12	
40	Residential	–	1	1	30	
Total		33	21	48	5,589	

Note: * from *NOIDA Yellow Pages*, 1997.

Source: *NOIDA Yellow Pages*, 1997, and field survey in December 1997.

Table 17.2: Shops' and offices' classification and numbers in some markets of NOIDA (1997)

Classification	*Intentional Markets*			*Markets Originated from Rural Settlements*					*Total*
	Gulmohar Sc. Sector 15	*Sector Shop Sector 15*	*Commercial Sct. Sector 18*	*Harola Mkt. Sector 5*	*Sohna Mkt. Sector 15*	*Chaura Mkt. Sector 22*	*Atta Mkt. Sector 27*	*Nithari Mkt. Sector 31*	
Clothes, belongings, etc.	5	0	28	163	34	65	313	38	646
Food	1	5	8	156	57	69	146	39	481
Bicycle, utensil, etc.	2	1	31	153	33	60	151	51	482
Others	3	1	9	171	40	41	71	26	362
Eating and drinking	2	0	5	7	15	9	34	2	74
Service shop	0	0	0	26	8	11	29	11	85
Service office	28	6	26	211	150	51	223	36	731
Manufacturing and repairing	1	0	1	112	35	11	31	20	211
Finance and medical	0	0	6	35	17	14	60	6	138
Total	42	13	114	1,034	389	331	1,058	229	3,210

Source: *NOIDA Yellow Pages*, 1997 and field survey in December 1997.

central areas, but this barely 10 per cent more than the number of shops found at Harola and Atta. Gulmohar Shopping Centre is extremely small with only 42 shops and offices.

Incidentally, commercial facilities planned by the NOIDA Authority are divided into several retail shop spaces with standard floor areas. However, in some sectors, the shop shutters are always closed and there are a sizeable number of vacant shops. For instance, the vacancy at Gulmohar Shopping Centre is 82.5 per cent, and 76.4 per cent at Ganga Shopping Centre. These commercial spaces are sold by the NOIDA Authority, and most of these vacant shops have owners. However, the reality that there are few conducting businesses, there is a due to the high rate of speculative investment looking for profit from future increases in real estate prices. As a result, even though the buildings are new, the shop remain vacant.

SHOP AND OFFICE WORKERS IN COMMERCIAL CENTRES

Next, we consider the places of residence of shop and office workers in NOIDA. First, workers at the planned central area of Gulmohar Shopping Centre are roughly categorised into those commuting from various sectores in NOIDA, and those commuting from cities such as Ghaziabad and Delhi. Of these, there are two notable points: many commute from Delhi, and many NOIDA residents commute from residential sectors reserved for military personnel. At the same time, workers at commercial Sector 18, one of the planned central areas, can be categorised into three types: those who reside in cities neighbouring NOIDA, in neighbouring Delhi, and within NOIDA. Of these, while those living from Delhi are the most numerous, there is not a large difference between the numbers of the three groups. Therefore, for each of these planned commercial centres, most workers commute from Delhi, while the next most numerous are commuters from within NOIDA who live in relatively luxurious residential sectors, and then workers commuting from surrounding cities.

On the other hand, workers employed at the spontaneously formed commercial agglomeration of Harola overwhelmingly live in the same sector. For commuting workers, Delhi is the most prevalent place of residence, and for commuters from NOIDA, those from medium to low density residential sectors or from villages surrounded by the industrial estate are prominent. The same trend can be said of Atta. Therefore, Harola and Atta supply goods and services for the common people, and there appears to be a tendency for many vendors to also come from the lower social classes.

This type of structure can also be seen in the caste of shop and office workers (see Table 17.3). Members of upper castes make up the majority in both planned and spontaneous central areas, and including non-respondents, members of upper castes appear to account for more than half of the shop and office workers. In addition to caste, we can see that non-Hindus such as Sikhs, Jains and Muslims are also employed in both planned and unplanned commercial centres. However, members of middle castes, Other Backward Castes or Scheduled Castes–the lower social castes–are not found working at planned central areas. We surmise this is because sale and rent prices for commercial facilities are expensive in planned central areas, making it difficult for members of the lower class castes with predominantly lower incomes to maintain shops there. For spontaneous central areas like Harola, and Atta, on the other hand, as original residents, it is thought to be relatively easy for even members of the lower castes to obtain shops.

This sort of difference can also be seen in the educational level of shop and office workers. Generally, shop and office workers in planned central areas have university-level or higher educational backgrounds. On the other hand, only about a third of those at spontaneous central areas had higher education such as a university degree. The majority had very little education, either having advanced to or graduated from junior school.

While the goods provided at planned central areas are of a high order, workers at shops and offices have a high level of education, lending to the appearance of a high-end commercial area. On the other hand, in addition to those with high education, there are many with low education spontaneous central areas. From this we can read that they are central areas with 'common folk' qualities. Class awareness based on caste remains strong in India, and it is expected to also have a strong impact on daily consumption activities. As described above, this has resulted in commercial centres in NOIDA providing goods and services divided into luxury central areas and central areas for the common folk.

FORMATION PROCESS OF COMMERCIAL CENTRES IN LARGE-SCALE INDUSTRIAL ESTATES

NOIDA is an industrial estate developed by UP state based on industry location planning the national level and industrial decentralisation

Table 17.3: Shopkeepers' caste in some markets of NOIDA (1997)

Religion		*Intentional Markets*			*Markets Originated from Rural Settlements*			
	Lank of Hindu Caste	*Gulmohar Sc. Sector 15*	*Sector Shop Sector 15*	*Commercial Sct. Sector 18*	*Harola Mkt. Sector 5*	*Chaura Mkt. Sector 22*	*Atta Mkt. Sector 27*	*Total*
Hindu	Upper Caste (Brahmin)			1	13	1	10	25
	Upper Caste (Other)	10	1	7	56		30	104
	Middle Caste				4		1	5
	Other Backward Caste				4		4	8
	Scheduled Caste			1	12		4	17
	Scheduled Tribe							0
	Unknown Caste	2	1	2	9	1	4	19
Sikh		1					2	3
Jain				1	2		4	7
Muslim		1		1	1		2	5
Christian								0
N.A.		2		11	10		18	41
	Total	16	2	24	111	2	79	234

Source: Field survey in December 1997.

planning in the Delhi Capital Region. As of 1997, residential land development was 45.0 per cent and commercial land development had reached 15.8 per cent of the plan. We must wait a while longer until the various facilities are completed, but from our onsite survey results, we found that these commercial facilities do not always function effectively. Certainly, the NOIDA Authority has placed commercial facilities according to a plan, and retail shops and offices can be found doing business there, but the occupancy rates for shopping centres and super bazaars placed roughly in each sector are extremely low. These shops were put on the market by the NOIDA Authority, and all are sold out, even the vacant storefronts. However, most vacant storefronts were speculative investments aiming to profit from the future growth of NOIDA, and many of these properties have not been opened as retail shops.

The owners of these empty storefronts are mainly private investors living in Delhi and its suburbs, or companies, allowing us to understand the extremely powerful influence of the capital, Delhi. The consumer appeal of commercial facilities with many empty shops is limited, making for subdued conditions for other shops and offices doing business, and the bustle normally seen in commercial centres is nearly absent.

On the other hand, an extremely large number of shops are concentrated in markets that have spontaneously appeared in the older rural settlements, with brisk activity. Before the development of the NOIDA industrial estate, these rural settlements existed as simple isolated villages surrounded by wide tracts of farmland. However, because this farmland was purchased by the NOIDA Authority for industrial estate development, it became difficult to sustain agriculture, and employment opportunities at incoming factories or in retail or real estate industries grew. As a result, shops and offices sprang up around these rural settlements, transforming them into commercial centres over time. In addition, the resident population of low wage earners in these rural settlements is extremely large, resulting in a shift to a 'common folk' market.

In this way, while there is planned regional development in NOIDA, because the rural settlements continue to pepper the site, this has resulted in the coexistence of planned and spontaneous central areas, two kinds of commercial central areas with different qualities.

CHAPTER 18

Transformation of Rural Community Neighbouring the Industrial Estate: Case Study of Village R

MUNENORI SAWA, HITOSHI ARAKI
AND TAKESHI MINAMINO

URBANISATION AND INDUSTRIALISATION AND INDIA'S RURAL COMMUNITIES

After the implementation of the economic liberalisation policies of 1991, the growth of India's urbanisation and industrialisation has continued to accelerate. Also, in addition to cities, the reach of the effects of these policies is growing and has slowly begun to encompass surrounding rural communities. Indian rural villages that had been dominated by the traditional caste system are also being transformed through the effects of urbanisation and industrialisation. To understand this, it is necessary to approach this in a new way, with emphasis on the local dynamics.

Urbanisation and industrialisation are thought to impact rural villages in many ways, affecting employment, housing, type of agricultural products, and the supply of goods and services. However, this impact even on a local level is not equal for all social levels. There are some social elements which remain unaffected by urbanisation and industrialisation, continuing in the old ways and customs.

Due to its location within the DMA and proximity to NOIDA, Village R has seen rapid changes. By understanding the urbanisation and industrialisation process, we reveal the effects on rural villages from perspective of changes in occupation and agriculture, influx of new residents, and changes in social structure.

CASE STUDY VILLAGE R, CHANGES WITHIN

An Overview of Village R

Village R is located about 15 km southeast of Delhi and borders NOIDA. Politically, it belongs to Dadri tahsil, of Gautam Buddn Nagar district, at the western edge of UP state. Due to its location in the DMA and within easy commuting distance to Delhi and NOIDA, it is a suburban village that has been greatly impacted by urbanisation and industrialisation.

At the time of our survey in 1997, its overall population was 1,175 people and there were 196 households. Residents of Village R can be largely divided into original residents and newcomers, 1,028 people, or 87.5 per cent were original residents, and the remaining 147 people were newcomers. Based on caste membership, original residents can be further separated into six groups: Brahmin, Rajput, Nai, Dhobi, Jatav, and Balmiki. As shown in Table 18.1, of these the population ratio for Rajput is extremely high, at 60 per cent.

The superiority of Rajputs can be seen in land ownership, seats in the Panchayat, ownership of telephones and electric appliances, as well as their high educational level. From these conditions, Rajputs can be called the dominant caste of Village R.

The age composition of original residents is a typical pyramid shape,

Table 18.1: Castes and their households and population in Village R

Original residents/ New-comers	*Caste*	*Administrative category*	*Traditional occupation*	*House-holds*	*Male*	*Female*	*Total*	*Average number of members per households*
Original residents	Brahmin	General	priest	13	50	55	105	8.1
	Rajput	General	landlord, warrior	97	339	280	619	6.4
	Nai	OBC*	barber	14	43	39	82	5.9
	Dhobi	SC**	washer-man	3	11	9	20	6.7
	Jatav	SC**	agricultural labourer	20	69	55	124	6.2
	Balmiki	SC**	sweeper	13	41	37	78	6.0
	Total			160	553	475	1,028	6.4
Newcomers				36	79	68	147	4.1
Total				196	632	543	1,175	6.0

Note: * Other Backward Castes, ** Scheduled Castes.
Source: Field survey in 1997.

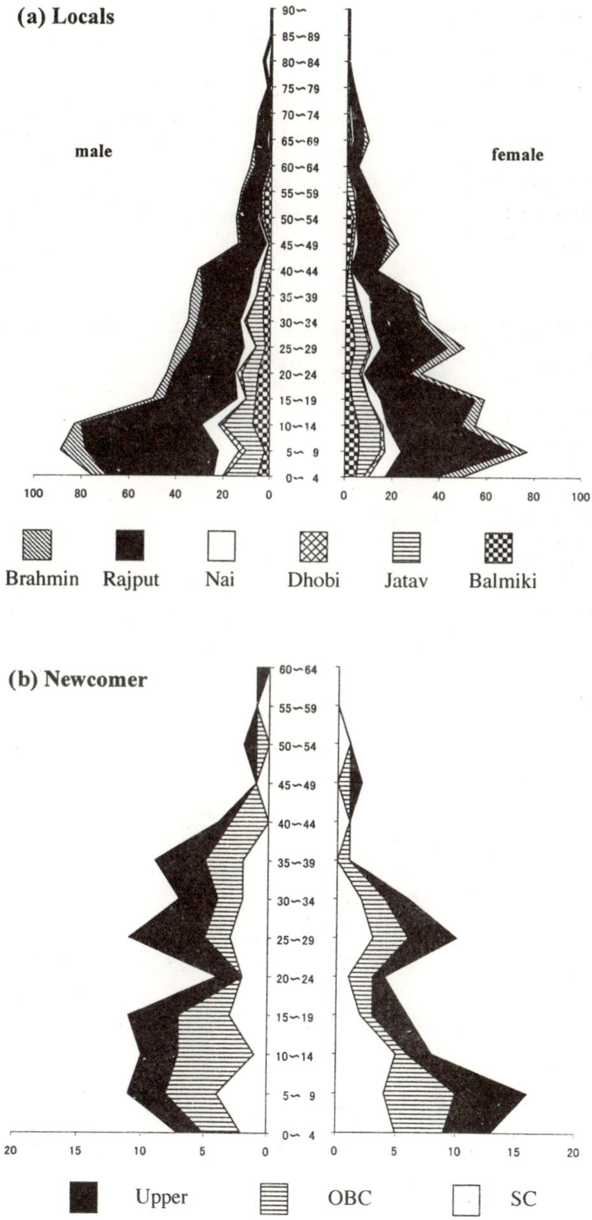

Source: Field survey in 1997.

Figure 18.1: Age distibution in Village R in 1997 (caste-wise)

characteristic of populations with many births and many deaths and commonly seen in rural villages in developing nations (see Figure 18.1). However, it is notable that compared to girls, there are extremely few boys over 15 years when compared to boys under 15 years. This is the result of the exodus of young men to Delhi Metropolitan Area for work or education. For girls, changes in population are mostly attributable to marriage, and a mass exodus like that of men is not seen.

Table 18.2: Chronology of Village R

	Major events	*Demography*	*Administration and Politics*	*Agriculture*
200 years before	• Original residents migrate from Haryana			
1940s	• Diversion of Yamuna River flow • Settlement is moved	• Segregation by caste is formed	• Panchayat is introduced	• Staple foods (bajra and jowar) • Sugarcane cultivation is started
1950s and 1960s	• Green Revolution (late 1960s ~)		• Abolishment of Zamindar system • Land reform	• Green revolution is no influence
1970s	• Embankment for the Yamuna river is completed (1976) • Construction of NOIDA is started (1977)		• Ghaziabad district set up (1974)	• High yield variety and chemical fertiliser is introduced • Sugarcane cultivation is reduced • Staple food (wheat) • Jowar as feed grain • Tractor is introduced (1976 ~)
1980s	• NOIDA bridge is completed (1984)	• Influx of newcomers	• Block Development Committee is introduced	• Watermelon cultivation is increased (1986-7) • Radish cultivation is increased (1989-92) • Fodder production is increased
1990s	• NOIDA bridge is strengthened (1992)	• Rented houses are constructed	• Panchayat is reorganised with neighboring village (1995) • Gautam Buddha Nagar district set up (1997)	• Agricultural labourers are introduced from outside villages • Vegetable cultivation is decreased (1993 ~)

Source: Field survey in 1997.

The Effects of Urbanisation and Industrialisation

Table 18.2 shows the history of Village R and the effects of urbanisation and industrialisation in terms of demography, administration, politics, economy, life, and social conditions.

The Rajputs, the dominant caste in Village R, migrated from Haryana 200 years ago and settled in this region. With the diversion of the Yamuna River flow in the 1940s, the village was moved to the present location and formed a residential structure segregated along caste

Economy			***Life and Social Condition***
Commerce	***Industry***	***Traditional Occupation***	
• First shop is opened			
			• Government school is established (1959)
		• Jajmani system is disrupted (Dhobi and Nai) • Reservation system provides government job to Scheduled Castes (Balmiki)	• Roads in village are paved (1982 ~) • Electrification (1988 ~) • Televisions are diffused (1988 ~) • New residential area is constructed (1988 ~)
• New shops are opened (1994 ~)	• Cleaner factories set up (1992) • Pen factory set up (1997)		• Government school is temporally closed (1992-5) • Private school is established (1992) • Telephone is diffused (1993 ~) • New building for private school is constructed (1994)

lines, as seen in Figure 18.2. The Rajputs have occupied the central parts of the settlement while the lower castes live around it.

The effects of urbanisation and industrialisation were not seen at this time, and the proximity to Delhi was blocked by the Yamuna River. Economically Village R was poor due to the annual flooding of the river.

Even in the 1950s and 1960s, these conditions remained almost unchanged. In the late 1960s, the Green Revolution was underway in surrounding rural villages, and great strides were made in agricultural growth. However, Village R continued to have low economic development. Because of the floods, the village was unable to make the large investments necessary for the Green Revolution.

This began to change in the 1970s. And the effects of urbanisation and industrialisation started emerge in Village R. The first impact was the completion of the embankment of the Yamuna River. This removed the cause of the difficulty to implement the Green Revolution; there was introduction of high-yield crops, chemical fertilisers, and well irrigation using pumps. Eating habits also changed, shifting from millets such as jowar and bajra to wheat as staple food.

The second impact was the start of industrial estate construction at

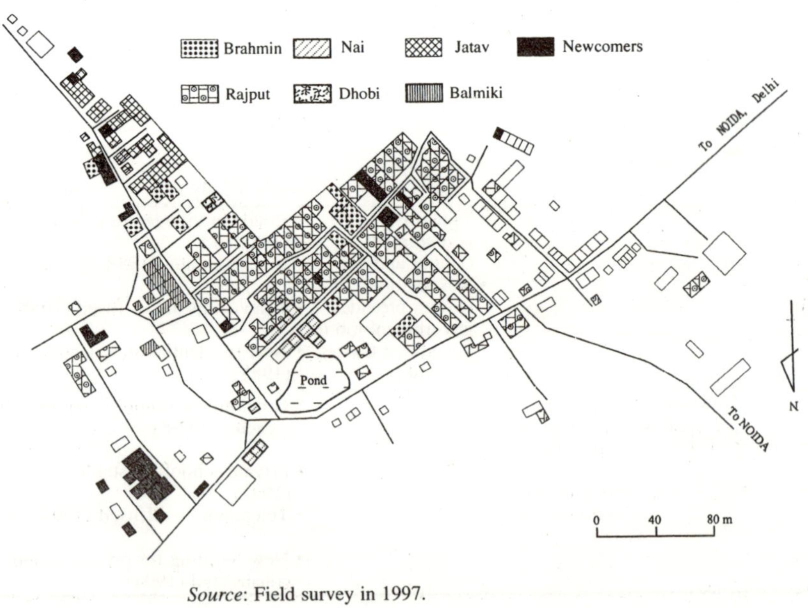

Source: Field survey in 1997.

Figure 18.2: Settlement structure of Village R

NOIDA. This provided work opportunities outside the village for farm labourers and members of lower castes groups who were unable to find work in the village except through *jajmani*. This was significant in that it weakened social restrictions rooted in landowner-peasant or employed-unemployed (farm labourer) relations.

The NOIDA Bridge, the third impact, was completed in the late 1970s. Delhi became closer with this bridge, causing more activities. The NOIDA Bridge was reinforced in the 1990s and it made interaction with Delhi greater. Moreover, the ongoing construction of NOIDA industrial estate brought growth in employment, the formation of a large consumer market and an influx of new residents. The effects of urbanisation and industrialisation on Village R were now becoming greater.

As discussed above, when looking at the impact of urbanisation and industrialisation on Village R chronologically, the 1970s were a turning point. The completion of the Yamuna River embankment in the 1970s, the construction of NOIDA in the 1970s, and the completion and reinforcement of the NOIDA Bridge in the 1980s and 1990s can be cited as three major factors for its growth. The improvements in land conditions, the emergence of a labour market and consumer market, and improved accessibility with Delhi contributed to the development of Village R.

VILLAGE ECONOMIC ACTIVITIES AND ABSORPTION INTO URBAN AREAS

Occupational Characteristics

According to Table 18.3 which shows occupational make-up in terms of sex and caste, initially we see a large difference between men and women. The female employment ratio (number of female workers x 100/ total female population) is only 15 per cent, far lower than the male employment ratio of 47 per cent. Excluding children, students and the elderly, most women are primarily housewives or work on family farms. Here, we can witness the traditional gender-based division of labour of Indian society.

Next, we look at the ratio of agriculture in economic activity. The ratio of agricultural workers in this village (agricultural workers x 100/ total workers) is 50 per cent, low compared to other rural villages in India. The high number of Rajput farmers is probably because farmland in this village is mainly held by this caste.

In non-agriculture occupations, public-sector workers, factory

Table 18.3: Occupational makeup in Village R in 1997

Sex	*Main occupation*		*Brahmin*	*Rajput*	*Nai*	*Dhobi*	*Jatav*	*Balmiki*	*Total*
	Cultivator		12	84	4		8		108
	Milk Middleman			3					3
	Permanent Factory Worker		2	10	6				18
	Factory day Labourer			6	1	1	2		10
	Construction day Labourer						1		1
	Company	(Staff/Clerical)	3	2				1	6
	Company	(Gardener/Watchman)	1	2			2	1	6
	Company	(Sweeper)						6	6
	Government	(Clerk)		7					7
	Government	(Gardener/Watchman)	5	13		1	7	1	27
	Government	(Sweeper)						5	5
	Teacher		1	2			2		5
	Own Business	(Shop)	1	9					10
	Own Business	(Barber)			3				3
	Own Business	(Sweeper)				1			1
	Own Business	(others)		4			1		5
	Other Jobs		3	18	5	2	9	3	40
	Student		16	126	18	4	22	12	198
	No Job		6	53	6	2	15	12	94
Subtotal			50	339	43	11	69	41	553
	Cultivator		1	52	1		3		57
	Permanent Factory Worker				1				1
	Company	(Staff/Clerical)		1					1
	Company	(Sweeper)						2	2
Female	Government	(Gardener/Watchman)		1					1
	Governmen	t(Sweeper)						2	2
	Teacher			1					1
	Other Jobs			3			1		4
	Student		17	93	10	3	18	9	150
	House Keeping		28	94	18	4	26	12	182
	No Job		9	35	9	2	7	12	74
Subtotal			55	280	39	9	55	37	475

Source: Fieldsurvey in 1997

workers and office workers are 16 per cent, 11 per cent and 5 per cent respectively, allowing us to see the variety of specialised work in villages near cities.

There are notable differences in non-agricultural work of each caste. First, Brahmins are employed as company or public sector workers, and as permanent factory workers. This corresponds to the high educational level of Brahmins. Possibly due to the large size of the Rajput population, we find especially varied occupations in this group. A common feature of the Nai and Dhobi caste are that they are frequently directly engaged in traditional occupations or engaged in occupations in related fields. The Balmiki also have a tendency to continue on in traditional occupations, but the reservation system resulted in a notably high ratio of public workers.

Inclusion of Village Economic Activities into Metropolitan Areas

First, we consider villager's relation with DMA from the perspective of agricultural activity. With the advance of product economy of agriculture, self-sustaining agriculture which was originally seen at the local level within a village or with surrounding villages began to fall in importance. Through the shipping of products such as vegetables and milk to wholesale markets in Delhi we can observe the inclusion of agricultural activities in the metropolitan area.

Large farmers taking advantage of its location as a rural village in the city suburbs in the broad agricultural market in the metropolitan area, chose vegetables as a commercial product, specialised in vegetable farming, allowing improved earning power of farm work.

The increase in disposable income that this brought on made possible an increase in the educational level of their offspring. Rather than government schools, they chose to send their children to private schools with better faculty, lesson matter, and educational facilities. Especially, some boys completed higher level education, and left agriculture to take high paying jobs in Delhi or NOIDA as public sector employees, company employees or permanent factory workers, allowing us to say that there are many who are encompassed in the broader space known as the DMA.

Also, outside of the upper castes like those explained above with high educational level, some village residents of the lower castes or Scheduled Castes took advantage of the reservation system and succeeded in obtaining work in newly opened public organisations or new factories at NOIDA.

For instance, members of the Jatav and Balmiki Scheduled Castes until this time had been primarily employed as day agricultural labourers, the lowest paying job in the village. But now, they have been able to find odd jobs such as gardeners, gate guards or sweepers in NOIDA, improving their cash income over their previous earnings. Through seniority, some have been successful in making the transition from day worker to permanent employment in the public sector.

This kind of growth in commuting and employment to cities and industrial areas has been a major turning point for the primary landowner farm houses who had employed low-wage Scheduled Caste day labourers originally from the village. Under these conditions, because the lowest paying agricultural labourers cannot be supplied from within the village, the landowning farm houses have to look outside the village.

Answering this call were seasonal labourers from the same lower caste of a village in a poor agricultural district with frequent flooding in faraway Bihar state. They are men in their late teens to late thirties, virtually all without land and illiterate. The social and economic standing of these seasonal workers is extremely low. Coinciding with the different timings of the farming seasons, they migrate between farm villages in Haryana state, UP, and their home towns. In the village we studied, they live together in huts owned by the well off farmers who employ them, and their daily wage is only Rs. 45. Some of them send a portion of their income to family remaining in their hometowns.

On the other hand, the two service castes (Nai, Dhobi) who work in traditional occupations such as haircutting and laundry originally performed services for residents in this village and neighbouring villages, but since providing goods and services to NOIDA and commuting have become primary, the weight of supply in the local space is becoming smaller, and the importance of a wide-ranging space is becoming important from an employment aspect.

AGRICULTURAL DIFFERENTIATION

Expansion and Regression of Commercial Products

Large agricultural change to this village was thought to have occurred after the completion of NOIDA Bridge in 1984. At the same time, in 1986, on the other side of the river, a fresh produce market was opened in the Okhla area. This promoted the cultivation of commercial produce for the Delhi market.

The vegetable production of Village R for the 10 years from 1986 to 1995 can be largely divided into three periods. The first period is the period between 1986 and 1988. When vegetable cultivation accounted for 15 per cent of all produce, and of these the main product was watermelon. In the second period (from 1989 to 1992), while in 1989 the cultivation of vegetables was less than 10 per cent, for other years, a high ratio of more than 15 per cent was maintained, and the primary crop shifted from watermelon to radish. In the third period (1993 to 1995), the percentage of vegetable cultivation fell below 10 per cent into a period of negative growth.

In response to this whirlwind change in vegetable cultivation, feed crops slowly increased to take over agricultural area. The cultivation area dedicated to feed crops grew by 1995 to account for 48.3 per cent of the total cultivated area. Most of this feed crop was used for cattle, and interrelated with the rapid growth of livestock and dairy farming in the village. The main objective of raising cattle was for milking, and the increase of milk production was thought to be related to the increased accessibility to Delhi, a major consumption centre.

The reduction of vegetable cultivation and increase of feed production was related to the labour force. In other words, vegetable cultivation required large amounts of concentrated manpower, but as described below, it had become difficult to secure farm workers in Village R. Some large farms dynamically expanded suburban farming centred on vegetable cultivation, expanding mechanisation through tractors, and accepting farm workers from outside the village. However, for small landowners who are common in Village R, the overall desire to farm was low, and it is surmised that this is why these farmers turned to production of rough feed crops.

Response of Farms

Including newcomers Village R has a total of 196 households, and of these 129 had some sort of farmland (see Table 18.4). Large farms are increasingly owning tractors and pumps, and growth of mechanization was prominent. Most of the top 10 landowning households excluding gentleman farmers, owned tractors. On the other hand, there was not a clear difference found for the amount of chemical fertiliser usage and farm size.

From the economic status of sample farms, we can find that wheat is the primary crop for each level; second feed production, which uses large crop area, is seen in many small farms; and third cultivation of vegetables is relatively more common in larger farms.

From the sample survey, the impact of development on the region

Table 18.4: Number of farm households by size of agricultural land (owned)

Size (bigha)	Number of households		Newcomers	Total
	Severalty ownership	*Joint ownership/ undivided*		
Over 50	3	0	0	3
Over 40	3	0	0	3
Over 30	4	0	0	4
Over 20	3	0	0	3
Over 10	30	0	0	30
Over 5	52	0	0	52
Under 5	27	7	0	34
Landless	31	0	36	67
Total	153	7	36	196

Source: Field survey in 1997.

was extremely prominent. Firstly, there is the appearance of cash crops which coincided with the completion of the bridge and river levees for the industrial estate development. Also, sorghum, which was the primary grain until this time, was switched with wheat, and seeing demand from Delhi and NOIDA, large farms began cultivating wheat as a commercial crop. Also, some small farmers could be seen developing markets for milk. For all of these, changes were brought on by improved accessibility to large consumer markets and increase in demand made possible due to nearby urban development. This shows that while on the one hand relatively large farms successfully practiced agriculture by producing commercial crops, on the other hand small farms had a reduced desire to continue farm work. There were some farms which continued to grow and ship vegetables from small plots, but there were also many with no desire to continue farm work. The growth of feed cultivation as seen in land records can be said to be the result of choice of many small-time farms that decided they were happy to only satisfy their own consumption needs, reluctant to engage in aggressive commercial farming.

CHANGES IN SOCIAL MAKE-UP

Influx of Newcomers

From social and economic characteristics, the newcomers to Village R can be grouped into the following three types. The first group is the male labourers commuting to Delhi and NOIDA, and their families. They have relatively high educational level, and live in detached houses in new residential areas in this village.

The second group is the male labourers living alone who commute to Delhi and NOIDA. They also have relatively high level of education, but many are also factory day labourers, living in this village because of low-rent rooms. They live in rented rooms at farmhouses in the settlement.

Finally, the third group is the male labourers living alone who are day construction labourers. As described above, in recent years construction of homes for newcomers and small retail stores has grown in this village. The educational level of most of these labourers is low, and they are from non-land owning classes in their home villages. They live together in groups in houses in the village.

The Collapse of Complementary Division of Labour

The collapse of complementary division of labour in our case study settlement can be modelled as shown in Figure 18.3. Before the progress of urbanisation and industrialisation, caste in the village could be grouped into three types: landowners, service castes and agricultural labourers. Labour, goods and services were exchanged between these groups in a local space. Payment for labour was traditionally made in cash, but payment for goods and services typically followed the *jajmani* system.

The complementary division of labour system that was common in traditional farming villages in India like this one would experience a rapid collapse with the growth of urbanisation and industrialisation. As described above, by introducing commercial crops, the large farmers who were the landowners improved their farming productivity. This income allowed some of their children to receive higher education, and by taking employment as office workers or permanent factory workers in Delhi or at the industrial estate at NOIDA, they succeeded to further grow their incomes.

On the other hand, those who were only capable of earning a low wage as traditional day agricultural workers were able to earn a relatively higher wage by doing odd jobs at the NOIDA industrial estate. Also, those belonging to the service castes were not limited to customers only in their own and surrounding villages but also came to serve the residents of NOIDA. The goods and services were paid for in cash and the *jajmani* system was no longer followed.

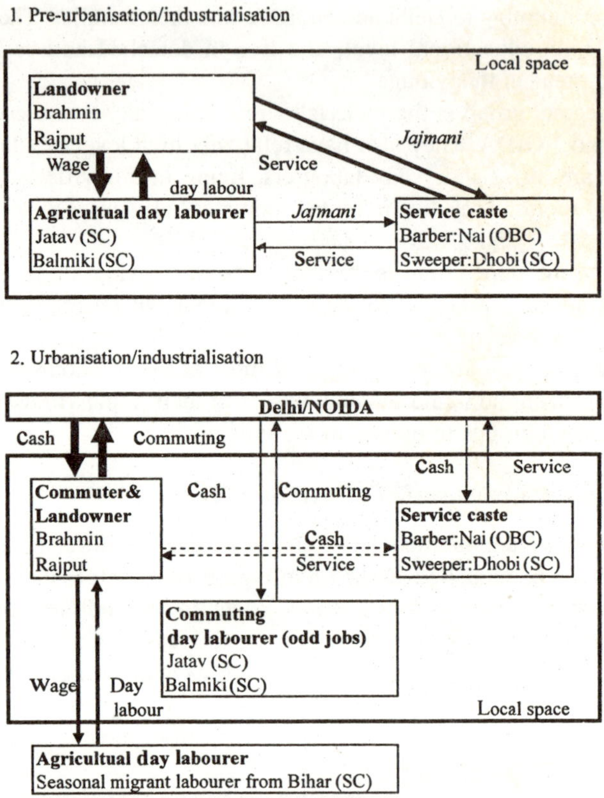

Figure 18.3: The collapse of complementary division of labour in Village R

The complementary division of labour system had existed in a local space based on agricultural production where the service caste supplied goods and services to residents of the village, and some landowners hired members of the Scheduled Castes as agricultural labourers. This complementary division of labour system is collapsing as the result of the villager's inclusion into the broader level of metropolitan area activities.

Reduction in Power of the Local Elite

Previously, the large farmers who were from the upper caste, as local elite, had a direct say in the determination of how to allocate farm labour and subsidies (especially Integrated Rural Development Programme).

Especially, when residents bid for this grant money, the inclination of the *Sarpanch*, head of the village *panchayat* committee, the local administration was important. Without their blessing, it was in reality impossible to make a request. Fuelled by the decision-making power for distribution of these two resources, local village power was formed around upper castes at the top, following the characteristics of the hierarchical Hindu society.

However, in Village R, farm labourers were no longer lower-caste residents, instead being replaced by seasonal labourers from distant places. Furthermore, with recent trend of *panchayat* mergers, villages with small populations like this one became targets of mergers, and were impossible to put forward a *Sarpanch* nominee. For this reason, the village elite, coming under the influence of regional politics, in real terms lost their decision making power over the allocation of grants in the village.

These two factors lowered the power of the local elite in the settlement we studied. The regional party instead is beginning to have an impact on decision making power in this case study village, as well as the capital of Delhi and NOIDA industrial estate. This capital is directly related to distribution of employment opportunity in this village–in other words distribution of wealth–for determining where new factories will be located, what kinds of workers will be supplied by the village, and how employers will recruit this workforce. Furthermore, when making these investments and hiring these workers, the industrialisation policies of the state and central government as well as the level of educational infrastructure (especially training for factory workers and technicians) have a major influence.

Changes in Education

There were two elementary schools in Village R at the time of the survey. One of these was a government school and the other was a private school. The characteristics of each school can be summarised as follows. The government school was backed by state aid and provided education at a low cost, but quality of inferior. The quality of education provided at the private school, on the other hand, allowed students to achieve a high educational level, but there is a greater financial burden on their families.

We looked at the student enrolment lists of both schools to see what kind of children are registered here. First, in terms of sex difference, approximately equal numbers of girls were enrolled in both schools,

36.2 per cent of boys were enrolled in the government school and 63.8 per cent in the private school. It reveals that a strong preference for the private school among the boys. This was a clear discrimination between boys and girls. However, thanks to the government school which provided an environment where an education could be obtained at an extremely low cost, this low cost made it relatively easy for girls to obtain education. It also made educational disparity between boys and girls better than before.

Next, we looked at caste differences. In both the government and the private school, children of nearly all castes groups were presented. However, when looking at the ratio, there were sizable differences among castes. Brahmin was 61.5 per cent, Rajput 77.4 per cent, Nai 55.6 per cent, Dhobi 100 per cent, Jatav 11.1 per cent, and Balmiki 12.5 per cent in terms of the percentages of each caste in private schools. Except for the Dhobi, who have only a few children in the village, there was a clear difference between Scheduled Castes (viz. Jatav and Balmiki) and other castes (viz. Brahmin, Rajput and Nai). However, a small number of children in the Jatav and Balmiki castes were attending the private school, even though it required a high tuition fee. This indicates that there were more opportunities for children of all castes to acquire a high level education.

CHAPTER 19

Conclusion: Industrialisation of India and Outlook for Industrial Estate Development

HIDENORI OKAHASHI

In order to understand the real state of industrialisation in India that has rapidly progressed since economic liberalisation, we took the industrial estate as our point of study and investigated the state of regional development from this perspective. In other words, by defining industrial estates as our field of research, without relying on existing statistics but on first-hand material collected by our own efforts, we tried to understand industrialisation in general. We summarise the conclusions under three heads: characteristics of industrial spaces and industrial agglomerations, characteristics of urban spaces, and impact on surrounding rural villages. We also briefly highlight the future issues facing industrialisation and industrial estate development in India.

CHARACTERISTICS OF INDUSTRIAL SPACES AND INDUSTRIAL AGGLOMERATIONS

From about 1970, industrial decentralisation policies were enacted, and industrial estate development flourished as a tool for bringing development to backward districts. Of the two cases in this book, Pithampur Industrial Growth Centre developed by MP government is a representative sample, attracting industry through various incentives and growing into the largest industrial agglomeration in MP. However, even though it has enjoyed external economies through its proximity to the regional city Indore, it still struggles with infrastructure problems such as electricity and water.

Situated in the suburbs of the Delhi metropolitan area, NOIDA functioned as a new home for factories that were forced away from Delhi by national policies for industry decentralisation. In this way, it is a large-scale industrial estate functioning as a part of Delhi, and for this reason it has many characteristics of a city such as suburban residential estates.

Industrialisation now reaches to the far edges of the Greater NOIDA district. Concentration of foreign-capital companies makes it a representative of Indian industrialisation after the economic liberalisation of 1991.

At NOIDA, under globalization, a new suburban space is being created through industrialisation and urbanisation, and is acting as a linchpin to clearly further drive growth in the metropolitan area. On the other hand, in a backward region like Pithampur, further industrialisation is not expected under economic liberalisation. It seems that economic liberalisation will further exacerbate the problem of regional disparities in India.

The industrial agglomerations in the two industrial estates studied, differ qualitatively. Many large factories are located at Pithampur, and it has earned the moniker 'India's Detroit' due to the large number of automobile industry firms located here. However, there is little trade between factories in the estate, the trade area is wide, and its weakness as a standalone industrial agglomeration is notable. However, we must also note that there are cases where the corporate headquarters is located together with the factory even in this kind of backward district.

In NOIDA, on the other hand, there are many small to medium size businesses, there are also many companies agglomerated here that possess proprietary technology. Also, there is significant trade between factories, allowing us to see that it is a highly independent industrial agglomeration. Today, industrial agglomerations are attracting attention worldwide, but when considering the future of Indian industry, it will be necessary to carefully consider the potential of industrial agglomerations like in these cities.

For the industrial labour market we only have the results of our Pithampur fieldwork, but this clearly shows the difficulty in labour supply in backward districts. While there is ample labour force to provide factory workers, staff are not sedentary in these backward districts, making hiring difficult. Also, even in new factories of this kind, we noted a large correlation between caste, classes, and labour market composition. The factor behind this is not so much caste-related discrimination as informal job hunting methods and educational requirements.

CHARACTERISTICS AS URBAN SPACES

The two industrial estates which we studied may both be called 'integrated industrial estates', encompassing not only industrial development but also aspects of urban development. This is especially evident in the case of NOIDA. This is because it was executed according to a grand regional development plan with a long-term perspective. However, these industrial estates reveal many infrastructural problems such as housing and commercial centres.

To meet the needs of the rapidly increasing population within industrial centres, commercial centres were developed. But both planned developments and spontaneous developments coexist. Characteristic here is the disparity of the commercial areas, and differences in infrastructure. Agglomeration is progressing in spontaneously forming centres, but this is related to the high demand for low quality products by residents. Also, old settlements are not moved but remain within the industrial estate. While the economic status of residents has improved, there has not been sufficient improvements in terms of living conditions. Residential development is performed in tandem with industrialisation, but those living here are middle-class residents, and members of the lower class excluded from development move into the old villages inside the industrial estates.

In this way, urban development is polarising into structures that could be called formal and informal. It is not clear if this is an intended outcome of government policy, but at the very least, the question of how to bring order in the informal parts left to nature is an important issue for future government policy.

IMPACT ON SURROUNDING RURAL VILLAGES

The impact on surrounding rural villages is markedly different in Pithampur and NOIDA. In Village C which borders Pithampur, the siphoning of labour for industry is relatively low and is not contributing to a shortage of agricultural labour. Commercial agriculture such as soybean production is growing; agricultural shipments are targeting the industrial estate, and there is increase in agriculture-centred economic activity. However, in recent years, renting of apartments and rooms for factory workers is on the rise.

In contrast, Village R near NOIDA is in transition between a mixed suburban and agricultural village. There are many jobs available in not only industrial but also public and commercial sectors, and many residents commute to Delhi. Farm automation is increasing to deal with agricultural labour shortages, and many migrant agricultural labourers are being hired from Bihar. One important trait shared by both villages is that in order to deal with changes in the employment structure, there was a clear change in caste and *jajmani* systems characteristic of traditional Indian villages. Also, with the popularisation of politics, the role of local politics was also increasing.

INDUSTRIALISATION OF INDIA AND INDUSTRIAL ESTATES IN THE FUTURE

Finally, we would like to consider the outlook for future industrialisation, and the growth of industrial estates. As revealed in the analyses of the automobile and software industries, sectors that have grown quickly since economic liberalisation prefer to be located near large cities. The sub-urban spaces around large cities are especially becoming centres of this activity. Through the introduction of factories mainly funded with foreign capital, an industrial estate like NOIDA which is located in the suburbs of a huge metropolitan area can be expected to experience extended metropolitan area type of growth such as that being discussed in South-East Asia today. This type of growth is expected especially in rapidly growing metropolitan areas such as Delhi, Mumbai and Chennai. While not discussed in this book, Industrial Town Manesar is taking form in Gurgaon in the suburbs of Delhi, which like South-East Asia, will not only sell lots but also perform after operations service for companies moving here.

What type of growth, then, will be seen in backward district such as Pithampur? Pithampur endeavoured to become India's Detroit by concentrating on the automobile industry, but with Japanese firms pulling out of the business in recent years, it is difficult to say that things are going well. Worse, there is an even stronger tendency for software industries to be situated in metropolitan areas, and industrialisation under globalisation is expected to bring even further regional domestic disparity. Hence, policy decisions for development of peripheral areas will happen sooner rather than later.

A discussion on how the progress of industrial estates in India will change in the future, and what kind of impact will this have on urban development and national land structure is likely to be the subject of future research. As briefly touched in this book, comparisons with South-East Asia should be interesting points for debate. Especially interesting is the comparison of rapidly growing metropolitan suburban spaces. Related to this, differences in urban systems and changes in direction should be subjects for comparison. India differs from South-East Asian countries in that it is not a development type that has over-concentration of industry in the capital city, but instead is notable for the relative distribution of industry among four major cities. Furthermore, a comparative debate on industrial estate development is important. In India, compared to South-East Asia the state and public sectors are the overwhelming developers of industrial estates, and differences can be seen in the methods of industrial estate development. Finally, while still not strong, an area of great scrutiny for the future will be how South Asia and South-East Asia will work together in the future.